AMERICA

HOPE *for* CHANGE

AMERICA
HOPE *for* CHANGE

— *Governor* —

BOB EHRLICH

Foreword by Rudy Giuliani

POST HILL PRESS

| CONTENTS |

| FOREWORD |

I am happy to contribute this foreword to Bob Ehrlich's second book about American politics, policy, and culture.

Governor Ehrlich's first book, *Turn This Car Around*, was a well received critique of how the left leaning media and their political allies seek to manipulate public opinion to their ideological advantage. *Car's* analysis of topical issues such as voter photo identification, union imposed wage scales, education reform, cultural identity, and the genesis of the mortgage crisis is particularly important today, as an aggressive Obama administration seeks to remake American capitalism and culture along hyper-progressive lines.

This well written second entry is equally important as it focuses on the issue of security in all its iterations. Whether discussing culture, economics, health, defense, energy, or retirement, Governor Ehrlich makes the case for a freedom-based approach to what ails America. His prescriptions are commonsense stuff mixed with a deep understanding of what makes America so unique in the annals of human history.

Bob Ehrlich is well known to followers of American politics. He enjoyed successful tenures in the Maryland legislature and the U.S. Congress. But it was his governorship of a deep blue state that caught my eye. In Annapolis, Governor Ehrlich navigated dangerous waters with aplomb and success. He transformed a huge budget deficit to surplus, passed Maryland's first charter schools bill, and wrote the historic Chesapeake Bay Restoration Act. Quite a record for a Republican outnumbered 3 to 1 in one of the most liberal legislatures in the country.

Governor Ehrlich is an excellent writer and thinker with regular appearances on *Fox, CNN,* and *MSNBC,* as well as a weekly opinion piece in *The Baltimore Sun.* Most importantly, he is a thoughtful spokesman for a party and movement in desperate need of a crisp, clear message.

Bob Ehrlich brings a common touch and clear thinking to a country in desperate need of both. His appreciation for the central role of security in our daily lives is a valuable addition to our national conversation.

I hope you will take the time to read Governor Ehrlich's second serving of good old conservative common sense. This is the stuff that will get you recommitted to a conservative majority. In the process, this book will increase YOUR security. Now that's a pretty good deal . . .

—*Rudy Giuliani*

| PREFACE |

"A person who publishes a book appears willfully in public with his pants down."

—EDNA ST. VINCENT MILLAY

They say the true definition of an expert is someone who has accomplished a task one time. I must be the exception to the rule, however: the process of outlining, editing, and drafting this second book was as daunting as my initial attempt with *Turn This Car Around*. Indeed, my respect for those blessed with the ability to turn out high quality books on a consistent basis knows no bounds.

Nevertheless, the strong sense of exhilaration that accompanies the drafting process has become familiar enough. It is a sense of satisfaction derived from the successful completion of a difficult task. In my case, the added attraction of contributing to the national dialogue on the most pressing issues of the day made this effort every bit as satisfying as the first. Of course, a degree of commercial success is helpful, too. All authors look forward to the day when one's publisher decides to order additional printings. Pleasantly, such was the case with *Car*. In this respect, I offer a note of sincere thanks to the many companies and associations that sponsored book signings and speaking events over the past year.

Special appreciation must be given to members of my Finance Committee, many of whom stepped up in support of *Car* in the same way they supported my numerous campaigns for public office. Their—and so many others'—willingness to back that initial effort made the decision to proceed with this one much easier.

On substance, what follows is the natural progression of the serious policy challenges chronicled in *Car*. The purpose here is more expansive, however. *Car* sketched a commonsense policy agenda for use in an increasingly politically correct (PC) world. It included a heavy dose of advice on how to respond to the aggressive intolerance of the modern left and its accompanying PC police. This volume explores the causes and remedies attendant to the seven most intractable issues confronting (and confounding) our culture and country: the role of government vis-à-vis the individual, strengthening American culture, fiscal practices and debt, healthcare delivery, job creation, social security, and national security. The obvious theme here is security: for ourselves, our culture, our government, our health, our jobs, our retirement, and our defense. The manner in which we handle these security challenges will determine the quality of life and culture we leave to future generations.

That we have differences of opinion regarding the way in which our country should handle these security challenges is obvious to all. What may not be so obvious is the degree to which modern progressivism has assumed a radically different view of these collective challenges. Here, it's not simply the familiar clashes of right versus left. Increasingly, it's more about a center-right majority versus those who wish to remake America in a stridently progressive manner. And nobody said winning this clash would be easy: the leader of today's progressives is the charismatic 44th President of the United States!

One of my former staffers used to comfort me during President Obama's first term by suggesting that in the same way it took a failed Jimmy Carter presidency to produce a Ronald Reagan, a failed Obama first term would lead to a Republican resurgence in 2012. But the theory was proven incorrect on November 5, 2012.

Talk about an unexpected result: a not-terribly-popular Obama was easily re-elected on the heels of a failed Stimulus, tepid economic recovery, historic budget deficits, and singularly unpopular healthcare reform. And it was accomplished by means of a grossly transparent campaign of class warfare, guilt by association, and character assassination. This time "hope" and "change" were nowhere to be found, replaced by cynicism and fear. The sum of which proved too strong against the handsome, wealthy private equity capitalist with the blue blood resume.

Our worst fears about a lame duck Obama were confirmed by an Inaugural speech widely viewed as the most progressive in many, many years. A re-elected Obama no longer needed to sound (or appear) moderate. The widely acclaimed speech (at least on MSNBC) promised a more intrusive federal government at every turn. This was the Obama of "you didn't build that"— fame propelled back to the White House secure in the knowledge he would never have to face the electorate again.

Amid the many recriminations coming from a thoroughly depressed GOP, at least one positive emerged: a re-elected Republican House is certainly a significant counterweight to an unleashed Obama agenda. But executive orders, appointment power, and Harry Reid's iron fisted control of the Senate will ensure another unsettling four years for those of us who wish to curtail the growth of government authority over our lives.

In these pages, I articulate the way in which American security in all its iterations is at risk due to an Obama-led resurgence of progressive thought and action. But this is not just the latest merry band of angry liberals taking advantage of a re-elected telegenic leader in order to grow government. These ascendant progressives are intent on remaking America's market economy and culture into something neither was meant to be: vessels for the growth of an egalitarian-guided government, where values (and value judgments) are degraded and the centralized state is celebrated. And they are making more progress than many of us could have imagined a few short years ago.

To make things more difficult, many of today's progressives do not share the security goals outlined in this book; their disparate constituencies (environmentalists, public sector unions, civil rights groups, feminists, peace activists) reject many of the baseline principles that define our system of democratic capitalism.

Exposing the fault lines in this progressive campaign to re-define America as we know (and love) it may cause discomfort for those who want everyone to simply get along. Well, such indulgence may sound good when you say it fast. And bipartisanship is always a big winner in public opinion polls. But going along in order to get along is not the answer for an America facing so many dramatic, nontraditional threats to its health—and security.

The political conflicts and policy arguments recited herein cover thirty years of toil in the public and private sectors, including public service in a state legislature, Congress, and as Governor of Maryland. Opinions generated as a result of campaign travels with the likes of President George W. Bush, Mayor Rudy Giuliani, and Governor Mitt Romney are included, too. Together, they reflect a narrative that can be frustrating, but always instructive. It is this instruction into the ways and means of contemporary progressivism (and what to do about its recent progress) that is the primary focus of this tome. The challenges described herein are quite serious in nature. Our collective response must be just as serious. The phrase "collective response" is used with purpose; *collective* as in majority, and *response* as in political action. The bottom line: my books are about far more than political analysis; they are calls to action on behalf of that conservative, commonsense majority most opinion polls cite as (still) the majority political force in this country. I have endeavored to set forth these challenges (and what to do about them) without "setting my hair on fire" i.e., resorting to gratuitously wild statements or headline-grabbing attacks in order to secure guest appearances on the cable news shows—or sell more books. This modus operandi may work for some, but not me.

Only you the reader can judge whether I have met my goal. I await your judgment—secure in the knowledge that an activated majority can indeed arise (2014 would be an opportune time) to begin an economic and cultural reawakening. It's time to get to work.

AMERICA
HOPE *for* CHANGE

INTRODUCTION

"America is great because she is good, and if America ever ceases to be good, America will cease to be great."

—ALEXIS DE TOCQUEVILLE

We have reached a fork-in-the-road in America. If we continue down our current path, we will diminish beyond repair our quality of life and culture, and that which we leave to future generations. If, however, we take another route—the more commonsense one that I'm prescribing—we can create security for our culture, our government, our health, our jobs, our retirement, our defense, and ourselves. We can dig ourselves out of the ditch that the progressives and Obama-ites have driven us into. Make no mistake: The time for action is now. Inaction, or just staying the course, presents us with dire consequences.

The health of our future hinges on securing America on all fronts. A great nation avoids policies that are penny-wise and pound-foolish. It honors its social contract obligations with its citizens. It welcomes qualifying immigrants but expects its newest citizens to learn and accept its cultural values. It pays its bills and does not mortgage the country's future through multi-generational debt. It primes its economy and rewards entrepreneurship to ensure good jobs for future generations. It remembers that Job One for this government is to protect its people from harm, either foreign or domestic. It recognizes that markets are far more dynamic (and efficient) than governments. And it supplies the goods and services required to ensure the health and safety of its citizens, particularly its senior citizens.

That America has fallen short in these lofty goals is without question. There is no perfect nation. We see the consequences of our failures in daily media reports. These shortcomings are the object of great debate in political races. They remind us that, try as we may, we have a long way to go in order to secure a strong and vibrant America.

But it is a mistake to dwell on the negative. America retains a special and unique role in an era of terror and austerity. The founding fathers got a lot of the important stuff right. Our social contract describes a unique arrangement between government and the governed. It nurtures individualism and societal responsibility simultaneously. It guarantees freedom of religion, not freedom *from* religion. It decentralizes power to protect its citizens from the worst inclinations of an overreaching federal government. It has generated a culture, for all its foibles and indulgences, that is the envy of the world. It altruistically sends its best sons and daughters to foreign shores to fight and die without territorial ambition. Its job creation machine is unmatched. Its standard of living is second to none. Its message of economic opportunity for all continues to attract newcomers from the far corners of the world. Its people live longer and are more secure in their retirement than those of any previous generation.

So, all is not lost. We have survived cataclysmic events, from world wars to a Great Depression—and have come back stronger, better. But today's challenges are sobering in their variety and magnitude. It does not help that we are led by an aggressively ideological President who is hell-bent on changing the terms and conditions of our social arrangements—not least of which is America's still strong (but diminishing) ties to free market capitalism.

At home, regulatory overkill, ever-expanding federal intervention, and a pro-redistributionist mindset are suddenly fashionable. The growing cultural acceptance of a larger federal presence in our daily lives presents new challenges to the entrepreneurial class. Employers fear the unknown and the wildly unpredictable, perhaps especially in national fiscal policy. Businesses both small and large continue to park their investment dollars and hiring sprees on the sidelines. A historic recession and tepid recovery contribute to a strong sense of economic angst. American-style capitalism is challenged to maintain an ever-increasing standard of living in the face of technological innovation and cheap foreign labor. And the American middle class begins to wonder if the quintessential American Dream will continue to exist for its children and grandchildren—the first generation since the Depression to have such consensual insecurity.

Abroad, the Obama diplomatic "reset" with hostile regimes such as Russia, Iran, Syria, and North Korea has produced precious few positive results. Aggressive entreaties to the Muslim world likewise have gone nowhere at best and negatively impacted America's influence at worst. (Obama's marginally improved international polling numbers as compared to the Bush era are his signal "accomplishment" to date.) Indeed, growing Islamic fundamentalism in the Middle East and around the world continually challenges America's grand experiment in pluralism and assimilation. Militarily, our cultural instincts are severely tested as an episodic, drone-centric state of war (incongruously coupled with a dependently non-aggressive and non-influential foreign policy) is maintained in a country grown weary of foreign interventions.

These are the battlefronts in our mission to secure and grow our uniquely American way of life. And as a commonsense majority daily engages in these social and economic culture wars, it is imperative that we take seriously an uncomfortable (indeed, distressing) observation about the loyal opposition: its underlying value systems are barely recognizable to the average American. In other words, an increasing number of today's progressives no longer share the commonly agreed-upon cultural and economic aspirations and premises that have defined our American experience over the past 237 years.

No better example of this new and dangerous value system presents itself than the collectivist narrative presented by President Obama and his surrogates along the 2012 campaign trail.

The president's aggressive rhetoric asserted that Horatio Alger stories (the very tales that have proven so inspirational to generations of young Americans) are indeed works of fiction; that nobody is a *real* self-made man (or woman) because everybody receives help along life's long and winding road to success. The narrative was succinctly articulated to enthusiastic response at a campaign stop on July 13, 2012 in Roanoke, Virginia:

> If you've been successful, you didn't get there on your own. You didn't get there on your own. I'm always struck by people who think, well, it must be because I was just so smart. There are a lot of smart people out there. It must be because I worked harder than everybody else. Let me tell you something, there are a whole bunch of hardworking people out there.
>
> If you were successful, somebody along the line gave you some help. There was a great teacher somewhere in your life. Somebody helped to create this unbelievable American system that we have that allowed you to thrive.

Somebody invested in roads and bridges. If you've got a business, you didn't build that. Somebody else made that happen. The Internet didn't get invented on its own. Government research created the Internet so that all the companies could make money off the Internet.[1]

Overheated rhetoric of this sort *was* scaled back as Election Day approached, but the Obama campaign's obvious enthusiasm for the narrative provided insight into how he viewed American enterprise and culture circa 2012. This anti-individualist mindset discourages accomplishment, rejects the notion of a self-made man or woman, and provides a convenient excuse for failure. To wit, one should not be expected to make it on one's own due to America's inherently corrupt culture. "The man" (usually not identified) will keep you down. Indeed, this is the "go to" narrative for many on the left—just too much racism, sexism, and intolerance to overcome. But don't worry, the federal nanny will be along shortly to make everything "fair!"

And herein lies the gravamen of the progressive mindset: it rejects judgment because it leads to disparate results. The consequence: a "cult of indiscriminateness"[2] lacking notions of right and wrong, good and evil. Nothing is black and white, just shades of gray. Hence, capitalism holds no moral high ground over socialism or work ethic over welfare-ism.

For this group, choosing requires judgment, and judgment utilizes values, and values inevitably lead to bigotry, privilege, and discrimination—anathema to this new breed of progressive warrior. It is indeed a convenient world where no behavior, ideology, or political system is deemed superior to any other. And how is this indiscriminate school of thought accomplished? Easy . . . just indoctrinate the young. The brilliant political communications pundit Evan Sayet phrased it just about perfectly:

7

[T]he elite does this by teaching our children, starting with the very young, that rational and moral thought is an act of bigotry; that no matter how sincerely you may seek to gather the facts, no matter how earnestly you may look at the evidence, no matter how disciplined you may try to be in your reasoning, your conclusion is going to be so tainted by your personal bigotries, by your upbringing, by your religion, by the color of your skin, by the nation of your great-great-great-great-great grandfather's birth; that no matter what your conclusion, it is useless. It is nothing other than the reflection of your bigotries . . . [3]

What a well-articulated diagnosis of the progressive's self-fulfilling prophecy!

That Barack Obama continues to sell this collectivist approach cannot be disputed, as he has reiterated such sentiments consistently throughout his life. To paraphrase Obama's former primary opponent, Hillary Clinton, it's all about the "village." And Barack Obama's village (and career) is filled with older mentors and friends willing to take young Barack under their wing. That these individuals were of an ultra-progressive bent is a matter of fact. The likes of anti-war activist and bomber Bill Ayers, Professor Derrick Bell, poet Frank Marshall Davis, and the Reverend Jeremiah Wright are but a sampling of those who mentored and influenced the charismatic orator and young community activist in the ways of liberation theology and progressive action.

The replacement of American ideals by indiscriminate valueless-ness proceeds unabated in the Obama era. Take the appropriate role of government, for example. Obama-ites interpret governmental security in an expansive way, not simply providing the short-term safety net a majority of Americans still see as the state's appropriate role. It was this worldview that caused Obama's Health and Human Services agency to issue its infamous work requirement exemptions during the heat of the 2012 campaign. Such is the approach of so many academics, clergy, and community activists: always more government and always-diminished individualism. These folks recruit others of like mind in order to bring about cultural change to a "broken" America they see as chauvinistic, racist, imperialistic, and greedy. The Lions Club it is certainly not, but more like a bunch of countercultural enthusiasts with a burning desire to expand federal power into every nook and cranny of American life. For them, it's less about a work ethic and opportunity to succeed and more about redistribution of income and federal preemption. For context, check out Dodd-Frank, Stimulus I, the automobile industry bailout, Medicaid expansion, and the unrelenting and successful campaign to repeal the Bush era tax rates on the upper class. Comparisons to European Social Democrats and their socialist brothers and sisters follow rather easily. Differences are there, but they are not material. Indeed, that a European-centric world view tends to cast a wide pall over the President's opinions is most probably attributable to American academia's well recognized "Europa complex" experience.[4]

What is absent (indeed anachronistic) in this background is the notion of good old-fashioned entrepreneurship: of self-reliant, innovative individuals willing to assume a reasonable risk in order to live the American dream; to take a path that *can* lead to the good life so despised by class warriors. This more traditional and conservative narrative emphasizes individual initiative and a demonstrated willingness to lose initially, but then to get back up and try again. The progressive thought that simply entering the arena is enough to generate a reward or a guaranteed result is antithetical to American competitive ethos. Traditionally and practically, Americans correctly view too much government as an impediment to success, not a preferred option whenever life throws us a curve ball. Hence, the strident opposition to Obama's policies throughout America's business-oriented states.

The security goals outlined in this book are not what drive much of today's progressive agenda. Fashionable left wing causes invigorate them. From the Occupy movement to Code Pink to the Service Employees International Union, theirs is a far different set of values for a re-made America. An all-encompassing entitlement state is their governmental model. For them, it's egalitarianism in lieu of capitalism's winners and losers. It's open borders rather than border security. It's an insistently implemented multiculturalism as opposed to all cultures within American exceptionalism. It's government healthcare over personal choice. It's peace rather than security. It's secular progressivism in all its glory. It's "hope" and "change," and an inexorable loss of individual freedom. And despite the reality of an Obama second term, all this must be reversed if we are to preserve our uniquely American values of pluralism, democracy, and market capitalism.

To be clear, by using the term reversed, I do not mean to imply a complete dismantling of the welfare state as we have come to know it. Indeed, some on the right have written cogently on this goal. But an increasingly diverse populace and highly complex economy have made Americans more comfortable with a larger federal role in our lives. This societal attitude would be nearly impossible to reverse. Truth be told, a large social safety net and significant degree of economic regulation are here to stay. Yet, there remains a significant middle ground between European-style socialism and a large federal government that nevertheless respects principles of federalism and freedom. It is this latter goal which should mobilize conservatives; ideological battles to re-verse the federal takeover of healthcare, high marginal rates of taxation, and Keynesian-inspired stimulus spending practices are but a few of the more recent issues of engagement.[5]

Indeed, such mobilization against Obama-era interventionism has begun in more formal settings as increasing numbers of state legislatures, governors, and attorneys general pass legislation or turn to the courts in order to protect their traditional Tenth Amendment rights.

The battlefield is crowded: challenges to federal pre-emp-tion regarding education ("No Child Left Behind"), healthcare ("Obamacare"), environmental protection (proposed fossil fuel regulations), financial regulations ("Dodd-Frank"), gun control (national registries and expanded background checks), and na-tional emergency response (FEMA reform) now litter state and federal dockets.

Here's hoping such activism produces positive results since there is no reason to believe this Washington-centric administra-tion intends to slow down. There are no more elections in this President's future. He feels no inclination to engage in election year pretense to govern from the middle. Instead, there is only an enthusiastic preference for feeding the ravenous appetite of Big Brother in Washington, D.C.

The re-election of Barack Obama most assuredly signals a turn away from traditional notions of security, both domestic and for-eign. At home, the progressives' version of a remade social con-tract will again be trotted out for social consumption. Increasing dependence will again be the goal; an aggressive, more intrusive federal government will continue to be the means. Entitlement reform is out, but diminishing welfare-to-work requirements, rapidly expanding food stamp enrollment, exploding disability rolls, and an increasingly provocative labor agenda will continue to challenge traditional notions of individual responsibility, fiscal constraint, and market capitalism.

Small business entrepreneurs will continue to feel the brunt of government's heavy hand. Higher taxation and regulation will make it more difficult to make a buck. And the reality of Obamacare will make businesses wary of meeting hiring thresholds that activate the law's more onerous provisions. This "triple whammy" represents a progressive panacea, but is precisely the wrong prescription for a more secure domestic economy, and culture.

In foreign affairs, the specter of a reflexively indulgent President makes us less secure abroad. How else to characterize a leader who orders a surge (in Afghanistan) on one hand while assuring the enemy of a firm withdrawal date on the other? What other way to describe an administration that declares its intention to create "space" between the US and Israel at a time when Iran is on the threshold of nuclear weapons and a once promising Arab Spring looks more like an Arctic winter? What better description fits an administration that refuses to employ the phrase "Islamic terrorist" in the context of the Fort Hood murders and the Benghazi embassy fiasco?

Opposition to this progressive tide continues to produce the oft-repeated indictments that seek to silence, or at the very least decertify, the right. This time tested Clinton-esque tactic (accuse the accuser, hard and fast) is straight out of "Progressive Politics 101." The narrative(s) are all too familiar:

> Oppose affirmative action—you're a racist.
> Oppose women in combat—you're sexist.
> Oppose abortion—you're the worst kind of sexist.
> Oppose gay marriage—you're a homophobe.
> Oppose multiculturalism—you're a nativist.
> Oppose gun control—you're a child killer.

But today's progressives have added a second element to Bill Clinton's formula: a scorched earth policy toward the accuser accompanied by a vicious intolerance. Add a complicit media and there you have it: a lethal cocktail of venomous progressivism.

Our last presidential campaign provides excellent context: select any week of Obama campaign 2012 and you will catch such attack-dog messaging. You see, in politics, when you're explaining, you're losing; and the Mitt Romney led GOP was regularly on the explaining end of progressive missiles intended to divert attention from a miserable Obama economic performance. And it worked . . .

The bottom line: a commonsense majority now finds itself on the defensive with regard to policy—*and* rhetoric.

An unpleasant reality emerges: America's security in all its iterations will be severely challenged during the remaining years of the Obama reign. And defenders of the conservative realm must be ready to defeat the worst inclinations of the president's progressivism while explaining its many dangers to the American people. No easy task.

All is not lost, however. A more secure America can successfully meet the challenges presented by the Twenty-First century. True security—of our finances, of our borders, of our culture—is not related to soaring, optimistic rhetoric. Such is a hard-earned lesson of the Obama era. True security on all fronts is dependent on the difficult policy changes I prescribe that will make a difference in the real world. A more secure America awaits that day.

| INTRODUCTION FOOTNOTES |

1. "Obama claims Romney 'twisted' his words on 'you didn't build that,'" Fox News, July 24, 2012, http://www.foxnews.com/politics/2012/07/24/obama-claims-romney-twisted-his-words-on-didnt-build-that/#ixzz24d51m6V2
2. Evan Sayet, Heritage Lectures, *Regurgitating the Apple: How Modern Liberals "Think,"* p. 5, May 10, 2007.
3. Ibid.
4. For an excellent analysis of European influence on the President's views, see: Mark Helprin, "Obama's Europa Complex," *The Wall Street Journal*, March 26, 2012.
5. For a provocative analysis regarding viable policy goals in an age of progressivism, see: "Conservative Survival in A Progressive Age," *The Wall Street Journal*, December 13, 2012.

SECURING
OUR SOCIAL CONTRACT

"The inherent vice of capitalism is the unequal sharing of blessings; the inherent virtue of socialism is the equal sharing of miseries."

—SIR WINSTON CHURCHILL

M yriad books have been written about the respective obligations of citizenship and democratic government in the United States. Countless scholars from the right, left, and center have attempted to delineate the rights, obligations, and expectations of citizens in this unique arrangement of representative government and far-reaching individual liberty.

It is not my purpose to add yet another analytical text to this mountain of intellectual history. That is the pursuit of professors, historians, commentators, and other pundits. Indeed, the proper role and function of government within a capitalistic, democratic framework is the fundamental predicate behind just about every policy issue presented to the American public. Think about it: the proverbial line of where individual liberty stops and government regulation begins shapes the debate on virtually every issue within the public realm. To wit, a sampling from modern political battles royale over the degree of appropriate government intrusion into individual liberty:

- Under what circumstances should police be allowed to record private telephone conversations?
- How limited is one's right to own a firearm?
- Under what circumstances should government act to protect the unborn fetus?
- Should marriage be legally limited to one man and one woman?
- Should government agencies be allowed unfettered access to one's body at airport checkpoints?
- Should it be legal for speed cameras to act as prosecutor, judge, and jury?
- What thresholds should activate government access to one's private bank accounts?
- At what age and circumstances should teenagers be allowed access to birth control without parental permission?
- Should an individual be allowed access to ameliorative substances in end-of-life situations?
- Why are beer and liquor legal and marijuana illegal?
- Should it be legal for mandatory student fees to fund campus political organizations?
- Why are Christmas decorations banned in the public square while Congress begins each day with a prayer?
- Which, if any, Constitutional rights should remain available to convicted felons? Foreign-born terrorists? Home-grown terrorists?
- What gives the government the right to take half of an individual's hard earned income?
- Should today's longer life spans dictate an increase in the age at which one qualifies for Social Security or Medicare benefits?
- What rights should illegal immigrants possess? Drivers licenses? In-state tuition? Welfare benefits? Voting rights?

▪ And, of course, to what extent may government compel and mandate the purchase of health insurance? (Well, guess that one's been answered ...)

The reader may feel free to add additional examples of complex issues presented by the dynamic tension between government regulation, fiscal reality, and individual freedom. And feel free to reference Jefferson and Hamilton; their disparate views of federalism remain fodder for the great philosophical debates of the new millennium.[1]

Our most important policy debates are delineated in the following pages. The respective outcomes of these debates will define the type of country we will leave to our children and grandchildren.

These line-drawing exercises are exceedingly difficult; many of the baseline debates have been around in one form or another for the last two-hundred-thirty years. Yet, so much of the acrimony around them proceeds without an essential underlying definition of our collective "social contract" and how extensive such a "contract" may be by government fiat. And the lack of a common definition to such an important democratic principle makes a majoritarian remedy to seemingly intractable problems almost impossible to identify.

So, what is a working definition of a modern social contract? Can we properly define its mutual obligations? And, can a working majority of Americans ultimately agree on such a definition in light of dynamic immigration patterns and changing sociology, politics, and cultural values?

An introductory political economy class at a left-leaning college or university might introduce the concept as follows: a cultural arrangement wherein the government agrees to provide the basic necessities of life and wherein such governmental support is guaranteed *ad infinitum* per an ever-expanding list of "rights" guaranteed to every individual—citizen and non-citizen. Such is the inexorable nature of an ever-expanding welfare state.

A similar introductory course at one of the relatively few right-leaning colleges or universities might define the concept in much the same way, but with two essential caveats: that such support be expansively defined to include non-governmental support agencies (non-profits, religious institutions) but be limited in scope and duration. This self-limiting definition implies concurrent responsibility to become independent of government largess as soon as possible. The essential element here being the familiar American concept of individual responsibility—a seminal conservative value.

This latter definition presupposes a more active individual initiative than many progressives wish to acknowledge. It denotes an expectation that citizens who utilize the government's safety net benefits (welfare, unemployment, disability, etc.) will quickly seek to regain their independence in order to make room for the next person in line. Unfortunately, this expansive definition of individual obligation has gotten lost in the Obama era rush toward European style social welfare-ism. Here, the dynamic tension between individual freedom and government has been skewed as public expectations about the role of government grow larger . . . and increasingly expensive—$5.4 trillion dollars worth of new debt during Obama I.

The Occupy Movement

Nevertheless, a historic recession has generated much progressive-orientated analysis around the need to redefine the modern social contract. The American Occupy street protests of 2011-2012 in turn excited numerous left-leaning pundits to offer their unique redefinition(s) of a modernized social contract for consumption by an American public daily exposed to this angst-laden movement until campaign 2012 and its own rather quiet implosion took it off the front pages.

Alas, in their unbridled zeal to [re]define our contractual obligations from a progressive point of view, most of the mainstream pundits chose to dismiss the obvious in order to search for the absent.

The obvious speaks for itself: media reporting from the left and right generally focused on the (very) loose coalition of progressive causes brought together first in Europe and then to Wall Street and other well known locales around the world. It was a political menu of every major known (and some lesser known) cause and/or grievance guaranteed to produce a mob: homelessness, Wall Street scandals, the "evil" rich, corporate greed, endless wars, green energy, endangered species protection, drug legalization . . . all had their individual support group involved in the extended sit-ins. Indeed, the unofficial list of seemingly random (and therefore sometimes contradictory) demands associated with the movement was quite diverse, and (for the most part) a little kooky to boot: free college tuition, foreign and domestic debt forgiveness, a $20.00/hour minimum wage, a guaranteed "living wage," an open borders policy, a trillion dollars on ecological restoration, yet another trillion on national infrastructure, a racial/gender equal rights amendment, pro-union voting procedures, guaranteed full employment, a negative income tax, repeal of corporate funding for political campaigns, "pay-as-you-go" military engagements, paid "sick leave," and reinstatement of the depression-era Glass-Steagall banking law.[2] Perhaps because of these disorganized persuasion strategies, decentralized structure, and disparate agendas, however, no one group or cause was able to convey a unified theme to a watchful nation.

As such, the assembled were eerily similar to other hyper-progressive crowds associated with civil unrest at G-20 and World Bank meetings of recent vintage. These rent-a-mob demonstrations are now expected whenever and wherever world leaders gather to discuss world events. Long lines of police in riot gear and the obligatory tear gas cascade appear as night follows day.

An observation for your consumption after dissecting major media reporting from numerous Occupy events: while there is a real and continuing sense of recession-driven despair among significant portions of America's middle and working class, the demonstrators of Wall Street fame failed to capture their frame of mind.

The reason for the disconnect is readily apparent when middle class values are compared and contrasted to the words (let alone the slogans) of the Wall Street malcontents: the rent-a-cause protestors' abhorrence of all things market-driven and capitalistic is antithetical to the hopes and dreams of so many Americans who continue to strive for middle class (or higher) economic status. To borrow a phrase, a clear majority of working Americans have skin in the game—they work hard and expect that their hard work will pay off in the long run. They do not, however, expect a guaranteed result, particularly from the government.

In other words, the familiar (and traditional) social contract guaranteed opportunity for upward mobility and wealth creation remains the primary goal of most Americans worried about maintaining their economic status during the present downturn. For the angry crowds of Wall Street fame, not so much. They recoil from the hopes and dreams of all those entrepreneurial capitalists who wish to take a risk, start a business, and make a buck. Maybe even buy an SUV.

Besides these wildly conflicting cultural values, each "side" possesses a quite different take on the nature of protest "demands" made to reach their respective cultural and economic goals.

From the Occupiers' perspective, the list of demands is tangible if expansive and unlimited: new jobs, a mandatory wage scale, free health care, retirement security, gender equality, a clean environment, welfare benefits, etc. . . . . Each requires a specific entitlement. Each enjoys dedicated support groups. And each is a familiar building block of an egalitarian society.

Conversely, the anti-Occupiers (for example, Tea Party protestors and their progeny) understand that government is unable to guarantee most of the foregoing agenda because it does not possess the ability to create the wealth required to secure the demands. Accordingly, their agendas are more intangible (balance the budget, pay down debt, live within one's means, etc.), but achievable, and consistent with traditional American values. This is as it should be—government's primary job is to secure the intangible (the opportunity to succeed or fail) as a function of merit.

The resulting conflict is obvious: the latter's more limited view of appropriate societal demands does not guarantee particular results—it merely allows one to compete—to "win" or to "lose". And that's not nearly good enough for the modern practitioners of class warfare-driven demand politics. Moreover, the Occupiers' social contract is completely one-sided; it contains precious few obligations on behalf of the occupier/protestor.

For a more literal perspective, consider:

○ One group demands ever more tax revenue from the rich; the other wonders why their "take home" pay is so dramatically lower than their salary.

■ One group demands government subsidy from cradle to grave, the other dreams of individual opportunity and success.

- One group demands yet another, larger stimulus and a "hands off" approach to entitlements, while the other sees Obama-era spending and regulatory excess as a major factor in our economic malaise.

- One group demands a new political class that will impose greater equality within our free market framework, while the other asks for a new political class that understands how such government intervention helped fuel our economic turmoil in the first place.

Some [still] contend a redefined social contract will indeed emerge from Occupy's summer(s) of discontent. If so, it will reflect a mightily disjointed value system.

Indeed, "disjointed" is too mild an adjective, as private sector organized labor proved to be a major instigator with respect to the "Occupy Wall Street" movement.[3] One is left to speculate as to what an earlier, more socially conservative labor leadership would say once informed their successors had gotten into bed with the most antagonistic fringe groups imaginable. "Aghast" would be a good start. You see, industrial-era labor leaders actively marketed the notion of the hard-working blue collar worker attaining middle class status. The "two car garage" and nice house in the suburbs became the penultimate economic goal for generations of such leaders and their followers. They were all about a romanticized work ethic leading to the middle class American dream, and they sold their vision to millions of skilled and semi-skilled laborers over many decades.

Conversely, the rabidly progressive Occupiers of Wall Street would be aghast that such conspicuous consumption could be viewed in a positive light: the last thing the green laden, no-growth crowd desires is for economic progress to create more growth, more automobiles, more housing developments, more demand for consumer goods, and more wealth in a country that already "suffers" (in their progressive perspective) from too much income disparity.

Limited horizons, confiscatory taxation, and aggressive government control is more this group's modus operandi. Indeed, a market economy with its inherent winners and losers is the polar opposite of what "social justice" adherents seek to impose on our country. For context, look at how many small business owners are represented in the progressive hoards of Occupy activism. Phrased another way, there were precious few work days being missed on designated "protest days." Theirs is a justice born of seemingly limitless government provided (guaranteed) entitlements—benefits that seek to level the results of marketplace competition, if you will. The bottom line: progressives' definition of social justice has little to do with our traditional view of freedom from government, including economic precepts of individual freedom, competitive opportunity, and wealth creation.[4]

Not so special interests

A further point pertains to the left's successful theft of the commonly used phrase, "special interest." Indeed, the phrase has become a popular pejorative among the progressive crowd forever on the rhetorical hunt against dangerous opponents. This hunt, however, is quite selective, as it is limited to groups *outside* the political left: insurance companies, Big Pharma, Second Amendment groups, and Wall Street investment banks constituting the first team of demonizable bad guys.

The flipside is fascinating, as wholesale exemptions for

left-leaning groups (even large, monied interests) are dispensed by liberal politicians and their sympathizers in the press. Progressive groups from the AFL-CIO to the Nature Conservancy to the Service Employees International Union to People for the American Way to Code Pink are protected from the ugly moniker. This fact of political life goes mostly unnoticed, as the newly aggressive left seeks to associate all things corrupt and negligent with private enterprise and market driven capitalism.

The un-seriousness of this dichotomy is reflected in the political giving of the supposed "clean" groups:

- SEIU is the fifth largest political contributor of any third-party group since 1989:

    In the 2012 election cycle, the SEIU spent more than $50 million on their favored candidates and causes.

    Since 2005 domestic labor unions gave more than $4 billion in political donations (an average of 93% to Democratic candidates).

    The American Federation of State, County and Municipal Employees (AFSCME) gave more than $57 million in support of its political activities during the 2012 elections.

It is beyond time the American public rejected the mindless, misplaced use of this highly demonized phrase. Just about everyone and every group in a true democracy is a special interest: one would be hard pressed to think of a job, profession, or vocation not represented in Washington today. And it's perfectly acceptable to advocate on behalf of your special interest. The right to organize and petition our government is sacrosanct in a free country. Neither side of the political divide should be allowed to ignore this fact of political life.

A New Contract

Despite the progressive left's provocative ways and a compliant mainstream press, I believe a commonsense majority of Americans can (1.) circumvent mindless pejoratives; and (2.) buy in to a common set of mutual obligations, despite our increasingly diverse and complex culture. Indeed, truly foundational obligations should be immune from the rapid changes associated with our dynamic culture. And so, three baseline principles for your consideration:

1. The country owes every individual as close to a level playing field as possible: merit based winners and losers should predominate. The American dream is all about the ability to compete [that is its *sine qua non*]—but never with an artificially guaranteed result;

2. Public policy must be flexible in light of rapid social and economic change. In this vein, it is vital to require policy makers to modernize essentially private sector programs (IRAs, 401(k)s, health savings accounts) and public sector social welfare programs (Social Security, Medicare, Medicaid) in order to comport with the way we live and produce today; and

3. Such modernizing measures should be market-orientated and freedom-based. The craving for ever increasing government intervention must be rejected, despite the best efforts of a dominant leftist intelligentsia to propagate the goal.

Diametrically opposed interpretations pertaining to the element of risk explain many of the dramatic differences between progressive and conservative value systems. Even a cursory review of the modern left's rhetoric reflects a desire for overarching governmental programs to mitigate life's ever present risks, dangers, and missed opportunities. And never mind the fact that the social insurance initiatives of the modern welfare state have not functioned as true insurance programs for decades. Pay-as-you-go Ponzi schemes (to borrow a phrase) are far more accurate descriptions of how these programs function today: there are precious few federal "trust funds"—the revenue just flies in the front door and out the back.

Calls for an endlessly expansive public sector safety net are everywhere and usually accompanied by the now familiar pleas for ever-expanding "rights." Indeed, a pervasive rights agenda is the new left's calling card: advocates for homelessness, federal health care, living wage, welfare benefits, unemployment benefits, retirement security, and gay marriage regularly invoke rights verbiage to further the notion that the new social contract guarantees them these and so many additional civil rights as a part of their citizenship, or according to some, their mere presence in the United States. Their ultimate goal appears to be a society wherein risk is all but eliminated. It disavows competition and its uneven consequences. It's an "equal outcomes" mantra. And it violates major provisions of what most Americans would identify as the traditional government obligation to equal opportunity, that is, opportunity to take risk, if you will. Thus, the increasingly popular phrase "Nanny State," an appropriate epithet that describes the dependency which appears to be the sole active motivator for policy support for so many on the left.

Besides the rants of the government entitlement cradle-to-grave crowd, there is a far more disquieting fissure among middle class Americans today: the heretofore unheard of notion that downward social mobility may be the new reality for future generations of America's youth. *The Washington Post's* progressive columnist Richard Cohen has characterized this negative mood as a loss of national "mojo, or groove."[5] And recent polling would seem to support the theory: a widely reported 2011 poll found that the proportion of adults who believed their children will enjoy a higher standard of living than they now have has decreased from 62% in 2009 to 47%. Further, a clear majority believed it will be more difficult for their children to climb the economic ladder. And, only 56% believed they have a higher standard of living than their parents at the same age, the lowest percentage since the question was initially polled in 1981, when 69% responded in the affirmative.[6]

The potential for this new, negative, national mindset to sustain itself for years is real, and the cultural repercussions are disturbing: upward economic mobility as an element of our social contract is essential to our confidence as a people. Indeed, the advent of a sustained middle class pessimism could inflict major damage on foundational principles such as the "American dream" and "American exceptionalism." There is little exciting and certainly nothing unique about downward economic mobility. Just ask the young people of Europe.

For example, young entrepreneurs might appropriately ask why they should work so hard when such an investment in time and energy is no longer rewarded—and no longer an expected (or accepted) part of our social contract.

The continuing viability of American exceptionalism is equally at risk: there is nothing exceptional about a culture that discourages risk and entrepreneurism. It's called socialism, or euphemistically "increased public control" and other terms. It's been tried throughout history. Its egalitarian promises are always high sounding. It regularly and spectacularly demonizes wealth. It minimizes market-induced risk and maximizes a social welfare safety net. It degrades the human work ethic. It creates gigantic bureaucracy and low productivity. Ultimately, and predictably, it (always) fails to improve the human condition.

Income Inequality

The foregoing facts of economic history are difficult to dispute, but class warriors throughout the ages have held on to one last rhetorical refuge: the specter of income inequality. This holy grail of the old and new left has attained ever higher status in the progressive tool box as studies reflect an increasing concentration of wealth in the top 1% of U.S. wage earners over the past thirty years.[7] There can be no more convenient fact for advocates of ever increasingly progressive income tax rates and government regulation.

The emotionalism attendant to cries about income inequity is easy to understand, but begs a logical question: what keeps the poor, poor? And are the wealthy to blame?

Practitioners of class warfare see direct causation between the two. In the words of conservative pundit Rich Lowry, President Obama and other progressives believe "some people are poor because others are rich." [8] On the right, the view is quite different: individual initiative, hard work, and equal opportunity (but not guaranteed results) are viewed as the traits that lead to upward mobility and wealth. They are far less interested (or jealous of) the fact that some have made it; rather, they wish to remove the obstacles on behalf of those who have not.

Nevertheless, to engage in debate about the realities of income disparity is viewed as quite dangerous on the right. Former

Congressman Steve LaTourette phrased the dilemma succinctly: "When you pit millionaires and billionaires against everyone else, that's a nice populist message, and we've got to get our hands on it . . . .I don't know if it's something we need to talk about but . . . it's something we need to be aware of."[9]

Congressman LaTourette's unease in responding to the powerful appeal of income inequality reflects a monumental challenge to the modern right: how to remind the average voter that wealth creation represents a net benefit to America without appearing to be insensitive to the needs of a struggling middle class. No easy task indeed—capitalism and its risk/reward system is *never* easily defended.

Two immediate responses present themselves if a common-sense conservative majority is to engage this charge in a meaningful way.

First, an honest review of economic history over the past thirty years. It is a story of how the wealthy have become wealthier and taken on a greater share of the federal income tax burden since the passage of the Reagan tax cuts. And, a story of how those at the lower end of the economic ladder have benefited from significant tax relief over the same period of time. They say facts can be inconvenient, and these facts clearly contravene the progressive's favorite indictment:

> *In 1979 the top one percent of income earners in America paid 18.3 percent of the total tax bill. By 2006, they were paying 39.1 percent of the total tax bill. The top ten percent of earners in 1979 were paying 48.1 percent of all taxes. By 2006, they were paying 72.8 percent. The top 40 percent of all earners in 1979 were paying 85.1 percent of all taxes. By 2006, they were paying 98.7 percent. The bottom 40 percent of earners in 1979 paid 4.1*

percent of all taxes. By 2006, they were receiving 3.3 per-
cent in direct payments from the U.S. Treasury.[10]

Of course, the termination of the Bush tax cuts for upper income earners only makes these calculations more progressive.

Any serious defender of this economic legacy must acknowledge the numerous tax preferences that have crept into our tax code in recent years. Many benefit wealthy individuals and corporations and give rise to strong (and legitimate) objections from the flat-tax influenced right and pro-taxation left. Nevertheless, no degree of progressive revisionism can change the fact that Reagan-Bush era tax policy resulted in the wealthy assuming a steadily increasing share of the federal income tax burden, while lower income workers have been incrementally rendered immune from that same burden.

The Numbers Tell a Different Story

A related history lesson corrects the progressive's false critique of the non-wealthy's rate of consumption and standard of living.

With regard to consumption, a well-reported recent study mined Bureau of Labor Statistics data to conclude that consumption growth across income classes has remained steady over the past decade:

> According to data from the Bureau of Labor Statistics'
> Consumer Expenditure Survey, households are sorted ac-
> cording to their pretax income: in 2010 the bottom fifth
> accounted for 8.7% of overall consumption, the middle
> fifth for 17.1%, and the top fifth for about 38.6%. Go
> back 10 years to 2000—before two recessions, the Bush
> tax cuts, and continuing expansions of globalization

and computerization—and the numbers are similar. The bottom fifth accounted for 8.9% of consumption, the middle fifth for 17.3% and the top fifth for 37.3%.

While this stability is something to applaud, surely more important are the real gains in consumption by income groups over the past decade. From 2000 to 2010, consumption has climbed 14% for individuals in the bottom fifth of households, 6% for individuals in the middle fifth, and 14.3% for individuals in the top fifth when we account for changes in U.S. population and the size of households. This despite the dire economy at the end of the decade . . . .[11]

More remarkably, Americans' standard of living (as regularly measured by the Federal Department of Energy) has steadily improved over the same timeframe:

- The percentage of low-income households with a computer rose to 47.7% from 19.8% in 2001.
- The percentage of low-income homes with six or more rooms (excluding bathrooms) rose to 30% from 21.9% over the same period.
- Appliances? The percentage of two income homes with air-conditioning equipment rose to 83.5% from 65.8%; with dishwashers to 30.8% from 17.6%; with a washing machine to 62.4% from 57.2%; and with a clothes dryer to 56.5% from 44.9%.
- The percentage of low-income households with microwave ovens grew to 92.4% from 74.9% between 2001 and 2009.
- Fully 75.5% of low-income Americans now have a cell phone, and more than a quarter of those have access to the Internet through their phones.

▪ One would hazard a guess that if you were to ask a typical low-income American in 2009 if he would like to trade his house for its 2001 version, he would tell you to take a hike . . . .[12]

As they say, facts can be stubborn things. Simply put, instances of super wealth may be more numerous today, but such wealth is not typically built on the backs of the poor. How then to process and interpret the attainment of extraordinary wealth?

Explaining Wealth and Poverty

My many social conversations in this regard usually begin with the mention of a famous wealthy person (Bill Gates seems to be a crowd-pleasing choice). The discussion proceeds as follows: Why should Bill Gates make (fill-in-the-blank billion per year) while the rest of us continue to lag behind? Subtext: it's simply not fair that one person could accumulate such wealth while so many remain in need. Any inconvenient citing of the philanthropic deeds of the wealthy target (Gates, for example, has given away an estimated $26.1 billion and has set a very public goal of a 95% "give away" threshold over the course of his lifetime[13]) does nothing to mitigate the damage, and not so parenthetically, usually does not get mentioned in the public discussion. Similarly, little empathy follows from injecting the previously cited fact that the top 1% of earners sustain 40% of the federal income tax burden. Bottom line: there is no sympathy for Mr. and Mrs. Gates (and families of far lesser wealth) even after the tax man claims a significant chunk of their income. No surprise here, as most Americans remain focused on keeping their heads above water during a prolonged recession and tepid recovery. In retrospect, the class warfare-driven Obama re-election effort understood this fact quite well. Yet, it is unwise for the serious person to cease critical thinking about how all this should play out in a risk-reward America.

For these individuals, the fact of income disparity within a capitalist economy is (1.) predictable and (2.) acceptable, so long as the wealth is accomplished through legal means. This notion is familiar to most Americans, as they chase an American dream defined by risk, hard work, and reward. Simply put, despite the rabid left's increasingly aggressive stabs at class warfare, a commonsense majority should be accepting (not jealous of) wealth produced by risk taking and a strong work ethic. An aggressive philanthropic activism is equally welcomed and fits well into the long established American tradition of charitable giving.[14]

I understand this is easier said than done as an increasingly nervous middle class eyes its economic future. And it is much more easily said than done in the context of a difficult political campaign conducted in a dark blue state against veteran practitioners (and exploiters) of class envy. As you have seen from my resume—been there, experienced that. Simply put, it is always easier to belittle success and employ economic jealousy. It is always more difficult to accept disparate economic outcomes—particularly in the political arena where there may be real costs attached to such public thoughts.

Religious Attitudes

No analysis of social justice within the context of a new social contract would be complete without some attention given to the role of organized religion.

The modern era high water mark for social justice re-engineering occurred in 1986, when Catholic bishops issued a highly controversial position paper on social justice within modern society. Many observers interpreted the statement as a Catholic response to Reagan era tax cuts or so-called "Reaganomics." As such, it became a cornerstone argument in the modern left's intellectual arsenal and a widely cited core teaching tenet against income inequality and other inadequacies of market based capitalism. A popular pejorative at the time referred to the economic doctrine as "trickle down"—the implication being that just a few crumbs might fall to the poor due to capitalism's natural affinity for disparate outcomes.

Cries of "economic justice for all" became a familiar mantra. And the rallying cry gained serious traction as a direct result of the Catholic leadership's (and other mainstream Christian denominations) determined efforts to change the underlying terms of our social contract. Common ground with the political left was easily found—both groups had determined that a growing middle class was not enough to offset rapid wealth accumulation on the top end of the income scale. In the vernacular of the Occupy crowd, the evil rich had become too rich, and a moral crusade against the wealthy had to be accomplished before things got worse.

The left wing of the Catholic Church is not alone in its determined effort to remake American capitalism; there has been a well-reported meeting of the minds between other mainstream religious denominations and the progressive left for years. Periodic calls for significant income redistribution through higher marginal tax rates on upper income taxpayers represent a common refrain. Such pronouncements tend to become more strident during prolonged economic slumps, which is a logical segue to the role of organized religion in an increasingly secularized, class envy-obsessed progressive movement.

Predictably, the left's most vicious venom is reserved for defenders of market capitalism and those people of faith who reject Biblical justification for an income redistribution-based social justice model. But relief may be in sight in the form of a newly energized, market-friendly enthusiasm among a segment of the Catholic clergy.[15] That this wing of the clergy is able to assume a more visible posture during the Obama era is no coincidence. The timely emergence of a well articulated, market-based interpretation of scripture is the needed response to the progressive movement's relentless campaign against free market capitalism. Indeed, a transparent viciousness directed toward practitioners of traditional faith, traditional values, and market success is a trademark of the new left's approach. And for those caught in the crosshairs, it is not a pleasant experience.

Eat More Chicken

There is no better example of this vitriol in motion than the left's treatment of the wildly successful restaurant franchise, Chick-fil-A. This popular family owned fast food empire is a high volume job creator.[16] And its steadfast adherence to Christian values—traditional marriage, nuclear families, a strong work ethic, and high moral standards make it an evil outlier for the forces of modern progressivism. Its official mission to "glorify God" only exacerbates the left's moral indignation. Its policy of closing all of its stores on Sunday drives liberal critics to distraction.

And herein reveals the true ambition of the progressive left: its theology of limitless government entitlements, secular culture, and egalitarianism seeks to redefine social justice in one fell swoop. Its message to the religious right: keep your moral and conservative opinions to yourselves. We are the only true advocates of a social justice model; we therefore are free to degrade those individuals and institutions who do not share our progressive views. A logical conclusion: notions of "diversity"

and "tolerance" are the Holy Grail for progressives in every respect *except* when it comes to those who hold opposing religious
and cultural views.

It follows that a traditionally conservative, market based outfit
such as Chick-fil-A would find itself with a big target on its back.
The conservative commentator Michelle Malkin characterized
the Christian giant's dilemma in concise terms:

> For the Left, these Biblically-based corporate principles
> constitute high social justice crimes and misdemeanors.
> Democrats are always ready to invoke religion to sup-
> port their big government, taxpayer-funded initiatives
> (Obamacare, illegal alien amnesty, increased education
> spending, and FCC regulatory expansion, for starters).
> But when an independent company—thriving on its own
> merits in the market place—wears its soul on its sleeve,
> suddenly it's a theocratic crisis.[17]

The targeting of Chick-fil-A is just one of numerous examples
of similar cultural-values battles being waged around our country.
The agenda (similar, if not identical, to the Occupy crowd) is
a loosely connected patchwork of progressive policy positions.
The tactics employed are by now familiar: boycotts, blacklists,
sit-ins, rallies, and online petitions. And the ultimate goal is to
bring about a newly minted formulation of social justice.

What To Do

The opposition wishes to rewrite our social contract in a decidedly progressive manner. This relentless effort must be revealed
and publicized at every turn. Each new progressive-induced

redefinition must be rebutted in aggressive ways. Each appeal by a secularized religious coalition must be resisted. Each opportunity to remind Americans about our unique cultural and economic values must be realized.

A deeper appreciation for the appropriate limits of governmental action will frame a newly energized social contract so vital to a confident culture. This task will not be easy, as the guaranteed media success of Occupy-type movements and the Obama administration's relentless attempt to divide the country by number of dollars earned gains traction. Nevertheless, it must be engaged if this great country is to prosper in the next millennium. Defenders must be aggressive in this most important of economic and cultural endeavors.

The succeeding chapters focus on the divide between individualism and government. My target audience: a consuming public seeking a political leader willing to draw meaningful lines and explain what they mean to the average American. This last point bears further explanation, as philosophical meanderings about a new social contract mean nothing to today's busy and just-getting-by middle class American. But everybody understands the need for economic security in an environment marked by unstable 401(k) balances, middle management downsizing, and weak employment prospects for many high-achieving college graduates.

Americans' ability to dig out of our economic ditch will determine whether upward mobility will continue to be sufficiently viewed as an essential element of the American dream. The stakes are extraordinarily high. Our continued role as an economic superpower and the chosen destination for opportunity seekers around the world is at risk. So, what *does* need to get done? Happy you asked . . .

| SOCIAL CONTRACT CHAPTER FOOTNOTES |

1. Hamilton's vitriolic battles with Jefferson reached new lows during the former's tenure as Secretary of the Treasury, as the respective antagonists utilized Congressional resolutions of censure and letter writing surrogates to impeach the other's positions. Jefferson even famously engaged James Madison to double team Hamilton on an array of issues confronting our still new nation. I am fond of reminding audiences (who often bemoan the "mean-spirited" nature of today's politics) that strong emotion and personal attacks have always been a part of our political culture. In this respect, I would agree that contemporary discourse only seems more aggressive given the real time tools available to today's political combatants. If thirty second attack ads on Medicare reform seem vicious today, just think what ads Jefferson could have run against Hamilton's positions on establishment of a national debt and central bank. For a good perspective piece on the hostility between Jefferson and Hamilton, see "The Feuding Fathers," *Wall Street Journal*, October 12, 2012.

2. Caroline May, "'Occupy Wall Street' Protesters are demanding . . . something," *The Daily Caller*, October 4, 2011.

3. Labor organizations openly supportive of the Occupy movement include the AFL-CIO, United Auto Workers, AFSCE, SEIU, United Steelworkers, Transportation Workers, and Laborers International. Lachlan Mackay, "Big labor occupying Occupy Wall Street," Center for Media and Public Policy (Heritage Foundation), November 24, 2011.

4. The transition from a traditional view of justice (defending so-called negative rights such as freedom from government interference) to the progressive version (limitless rights to government entitlements) has been analyzed by numerous commentators in recent decades.

5. Richard Cohen, "A Downwardly Mobile Nation," *The Washington Post*, September 19, 2011.

6. Pew Charitable Trust- Economic Mobility Project, "Economic Mobility and the American Dream: Where Do We Stand in the Wake of

the Great Recession?" www.economicmobility.org/poll2011, May 19, 2011.

7. A widely-reported Congressional Budget Office report in October 2011 reflected that average household income for the top 1% of wage earners increased 275% from 1979 to 2007 while the bottom 20% saw just an 18% increase over the same timeframe.

8. Rich Lowry, "Blame the rich for inequality," *The National Review,* December 8, 2011.

9. Marin Cogan and Jake Sherman, "Income Gap Slips Into the GOP Line," *Politico,* October 31, 2011.

10. Former U.S. Senator Phil Graham, "Reaganomics and the American Character," *Imprints,* (A publication of Hillsdale College), November, 2011.

11. Keven A. Hassatt and Aparna Mathura, "Consumption and the Myths of Inequality," *The Wall Street Journal,* October 2012.

12. Ibid.

13. www.billgatesmicrosoft.com/networth.htm / www.learningtogive. org

14. Philanthropic giving in America continues to grow, despite the historic recession of 2007-2009. In 2010 a fragile recovery and uneven stock market did not stop American individuals, corporations, and foundations from giving an estimated $290 billion to charities of all stripes. Giving USA Foundation, The Center on Philanthropy, June 20, 2011.

15. See: Rev. Robert Sirico, "Defending the Free Market: The Moral Case for a Free Economy," (Regnery Publishing, Inc.), 2012.

16. Chick-fil-a employs 50,000 workers at 1500 outlets around the country: Michelle Malkin, "A Christian Business in the Left's Crosshairs," February 2, 2011.

17. Michelle Maklin, "Stop the hate campaign against law-abiding American businesses," *michellemalkin.com,* February 2, 2011.

OUR UNSECURED
FISCAL FUTURE

"And to preserve their independence, we must
not let our rulers load us with perpetual debt.
We must make our election between economy
and liberty, or profusion and servitude."

—THOMAS JEFFERSON

F or a nation that tends to celebrate grassroots movements, the hostility generated and directed toward the Tea Party uprising—regular citizens standing up against out-of-control government spending—has been quite perplexing, but not so surprising, especially when juxtaposed with the much celebrated Occupy Wall Street, which demanded the exact opposite. After all, these activists were (are) serious about changing the economic landscape presently overseen by the Obama Administration, the one where heavy-handed government spending and the over-taxing of wealth is never enough; where class warfare has reached its boiling point. Indeed, this movement is all about ringing the fiscal alarm bells, even if the Obama progressives care not to listen. Speaking of which, by the time you finish reading this chapter the federal deficit will have grown by $23 million.

Think back to the 2010 mid-term elections when profligate federal spending was the focal point. Public frustration with an underperforming economy and trillions in new debt brought Republican control to the House of Representatives. Many of these new budget hawks arrived on Capitol Hill with a Tea Party imprimatur and willingness—indeed an eagerness—to challenge the town's cultural spending habits. A new movement had been born, and Tea Party economics was soon seen to be a very real threat to the status quo.

Immediately, America's left-leaning media machine and progressive interest groups sprang into action. A furious negative critique was directed at the interlopers. Almost daily, the *Washington Post's* editorial pages were full of grand indictments against all things Tea Party, the GOP Congress, or the leading Republican presidential contenders.

The editorial headlines reflected the unbridled vitriol: "Those Reckless Republicans," "The Tea Party, united only by Anger and the Internet," "Conservative Zealotry vs. Economic Reality," "Racism and the Tea Party Movement," and "The GOP's Carjacking on Capitol Hill." Such is just a sampling of reviews produced by the left wing establishment's opinion makers in the aftermath of the 2010 mid-term elections and the emergence of a Tea Party-driven fiscal agenda within the Congressional GOP.

The Washington establishment was in a bad mood, a negative mindset that only got worse as each passing day brought its share of disquieting economic news.

Hot Politicians and Brief Honeymoons

What brought about such an ugly state of affairs? Why was mainstream media coverage of one of the few major interest groups serious about our nation's mind-numbing debt so presumptively and predicatively negative, even vicious in its coverage? And what did the average Tea Party protestor/tax activist *do* to deserve such dismissive treatment from so many leading opinion makers?

Well, after two decades in the political arena, I believe the answers are readily apparent, but one has to care to look. First, the rapid downturn in the President's poll numbers after the euphoria of early 2009 was not an easy thing to watch, even for many conservatives. Most of us on the right want the best outcomes for the country, regardless of whether the president is of the other party. Nevertheless, it didn't take long for the widely proclaimed post-partisan "leader of leaders" to be seen as what many of us thought he was: a traditional liberal (albeit an attractive, personally likeable and telegenic one) who has advocated mostly traditional liberal remedies for what ails America. Worse, such advocacy has usually been delivered from behind, as Congressional Democratic leaders took it upon themselves to fill in the details of the President's self-proclaimed signature first term legislative accomplishments: Stimulus and Obamacare.

Political pundits rarely report on the mechanics of why so many charismatic politicians fail to stay popular over time. The extreme difficulty is reflected in recent presidential experience: besides Obama, one need look no further than President George H.W. Bush's short-lived 90 percent approval rating post Gulf War I and President George W. Bush's similar approval rating in the aftermath of 9/11.

Two primary facts of political life explain this pattern. One, even monumental events (9/11, victory in WWII, killing bin Laden) have limited shelf lives; a scandal or recession often serves to curtail euphoric notions of long-term approval in modern democracies. As they say, life unfolds daily, bringing with it a regular dose of human foibles and problematic economic developments.

The second element pertains to those relatively rare chapters wherein political leaders attain unparalleled heights of popularity due to a strong ideological bent. These philosophical leaders often energize their political base in highly charged ways. Those followers achieve an unnatural and impossible to sustain degree of intensive enthusiasm for the leader and his or her agenda. Here again, daily life unfolds—as the realities of limited executive authority, a combative opposition, periodic scandal, the cyclical nature of the economy, or taking a position on a divisive social issue begin to wear down the most popular politician. The added drama of a cyberspace induced 24/7 news-cycle only further exacerbates the challenge of maintaining consistently high poll numbers. In addition, public opinion polls rarely delve into poll instability, a phenomenon wherein great initial success is followed by raised expectations, which inevitably are unrealized, or there occurs a newly discovered chink in the armor, causing doubt wherein little previously existed. It's why so many popular businessmen, athletes, and actors have enjoyed only limited success in politics. Everybody might love the guy who scored thirty touchdowns last year; half the voters will be far less enthusiastic once that same athlete declares himself "pro-life" or "pro-choice." And what about gun control and capital punishment and marriage and stem cell research and the next bitterly divisive social issue that comes down the pike? The most inconvenient fact of political life: all-intensive majoritarian support is unstable over time. Even FDR's waned considerably into his fourth term.[1]

Yet another reason for the left's (tempered) discontent: a willingness to keep Bush era security policies in place. Gitmo remains open, rendition of enemy combatants continues to occur, and the number of drone attacks against terrorist leaders has far surpassed the Bush administration's record. Indeed, it is the most progressive of Presidents who has demonstrated a willingness to kill American citizens in secret—a policy repulsive to the left's leading interest groups during the Bush era.

The tone and tenor of the campaign in 2012 is another case in point. Although Obama won a second term, the campaign clearly lacked the inspirational enthusiasm of the first. Gone was the candidate of "hope" and "change." This was a more traditional and some might say "Chicago style" fight with a focus on relentlessly negative ads aimed at Mitt Romney's wealth and business experience. Progressive support for Obama should not mask the general public's, and even some of the left's, real sense of disappointment that the modern era's most left-leaning president failed to turn around a morbid economy. The economic facts were ugly and difficult to dismiss: a lethal cocktail of negligently applied stimulus, massive federal intervention in our healthcare delivery system, and highly aggressive regulatory regimes did little to revive an economy still reeling from a mortgage crisis-induced recession. And it is difficult to find any economist willing to predict a dramatic turnaround anytime in the near future.

Indeed, "ugly" may be too tepid a term: sustained unemployment in excess of seven percent, lackluster consumer confidence, and an unwillingness to tackle a $17 trillion debt is enough to dampen even the most optimistic partisan's outlook.

The Unhappy Progressive

One must understand the progressive worldview at work here. It can accept only one type of populism. This brand is the traditional nineteenth century variety: it speaks to "evil" multinational corporations, class warfare, and centralized remedies for all that ails us. As such, it is the polar opposite of a "new" right-leaning populism targeting confiscatory taxation, over-regulation, rampant unionism, and a "Washington knows best" mindset.

The traditional approach was brilliantly employed by Senator Obama in 2008, and then-President Obama in 2012. The strategy was perfect for the time: an unpopular GOP, continuing middle class anxiety, a Wall Street-inspired recession, and two unpopular wars made for a receptive audience and a willingness to put aside concerns about the Senator from Illinois' hyper-progressive views and lack of executive experience. Indeed, the polished Obama had it *both* ways. His aggressively anti-Wall Street rhetoric backed up by a dismal anti-business voting record in two legislatures was rewarded with big Wall Street money, at least during his initial run. Goldman Sachs employees led the money parade, contributing more than one million dollars during the 2008 election cycle.[2] But by 2012 even Wall Street tired of getting beaten up; "the Street" leaned toward Romney and the GOP the second time around.[3]

Life Between the Coasts

It is the makeup of the Tea Party protesters that generates the most hostility—you see, they tend to live between the coasts, in "fly-over America." These states trend red on Election Day. This protest movement's rhetoric is steeped in a new libertarian-influenced populism—more anti-government, anti-Washington, anti-tax, and anti-federal preemption than past incarnations of conservative-inspired realignments. Moreover, component parts of the movement seem far less vexed by the relentless tide of hyper-aggressive criticism emanating from Washington's opinion maker establishment.[4] As such, they represent a more direct challenge to those who are vested in gigantic government presently overseen by Obama-era installed czars focused on the expansion of federal control into every nook and cranny of American life.

Not Nearly Liberal Enough

A closer examination of the left's indictments against the Obama record reflects disappointment about the administration's failure to do more: more regulation, more taxes, more federal preemption, and more government control of American life. The refrain is familiar: if only that $1.2 trillion stimulus could have been larger, if only another major stimulus could pass, if only those dogmatic Republicans would agree to higher taxes, if only the country would understand the need for ever-additional revenue to stock the federal coffers . . .

Witness the protestations of Vice President Biden in August of 2011: "I think the economy does need more stimulus . . . Everybody says we should've (had) . . . a bigger stimulus package. Yeah, we should've. I was pushing (for) it."[5]

Or, the remorseful tone of liberal columnist Richard Cohen as he joylessly endorsed another Obama term in the White House:

"[S]omewhere between the campaign and the White House itself, Obama got lost. It turned out he had no cause at all. Expanding health insurance was Hillary Clinton's longtime goal, and even after Obama adopted it, he never argued for it with any fervor . . . [W]hen he took office, climate change was abandoned—too much trouble, too much opposition . . . Obama never espoused a cause bigger than his own political survival."[6]

Yes, you read that correctly: the most free spending president in history, the man who undertook to control 16 percent of the American economy through a $1 trillion healthcare bill—that man had "no cause at all."

Hopefully, most Americans have figured out this "more is never enough" narrative is economically incoherent, but mandatory on the left. The plaintive criticisms are incorrect because more progressive tax rates on upper income earners neither raise much (new) revenue nor help the economy grow. Higher and more complex tax burdens mostly serve the interests of tax lawyers and accountants, not the poor. In a philosophical sense, however, the critiques are mandatory because they provide an "out" for true believers. The readily available and never disprovable excuse of "if only they could have done more" eliminates confrontation with the dreaded ultimate conclusion: what progressives believe does not work well in the real world. For this group, far better to believe that a world full of endless needs ("investments") necessitates endless federal spending. The baseline legitimacy of the needs makes the case even stronger as most Americans at initial impression appear to support increasing federal spending on unemployment benefits, food stamps, and bio-fuel research—not to mention The Big Three: Medicare, Medicaid, and Social Security.

Most popular opinion polls reflect these somewhat reflexive attitudes but lack substantial follow-up questions and responses as to the appropriate duration and generosity of these benefits. For context, there is little doubt that most Americans support unemployment benefits for those who lose their jobs. It is quite a different notion to support the extension of such benefits for ninety-nine weeks. Yet, further extensions are always a progressive "ask" during Congressional budget negotiations.

A first cousin to "more" is "demand," for what good would more government goodies be if not the result of aggressive demands from the left? And what better example presents itself than the Occupy movement's focus on the demand for millions of new jobs, all with a "living wage" and accompanying benefits, of course. The elementary truth that government is unable to create these mythical jobs did not register with the policy-ignorant on the local corner, since new jobs are just one of the "more" family—a group with seemingly limitless expectations.

The Effective Demagogue

The "never enough" rhetoric also serves as a predicate for the left's "go to" rejoinder whenever and wherever redistributionist initiatives fail: class warfare. And there has been no better tactician in this respect than Barack Obama. Witness the classic rhetoric at the Silicon Valley headquarters of Facebook in September, 2011:

"But I think that what he [Rep. Paul Ryan] and the other Republicans in the House of Representatives also want to do is change our social compact in a pretty fundamental way. Their basic view is that no matter how successful I am, no matter how much I've taken from this country—I wasn't born wealthy; I was raised by a single mom and my grandparents; I went to college on scholarships. There was a time when my mom was trying to get her PhD, where for a short time she had to take food stamps. My grandparents relied on Medicare and Social Security to help supplement their income when they got old. So their notion is, despite the fact that I've benefited from all these investments—my grandfather benefited from the GI Bill after he fought in World War II—that somehow I now have no obligation to people who are less fortunate than me and I have no real obligation to future generations to make investments so that they have a better [future]."[7]

Forget for a moment the intellectual emptiness of a straw man who lacks any sense of social responsibility. Focus on the emotional appeal instead. It's pretty powerful, and made more so by the myriad devil-figure targets available to purveyors of class warfare rhetoric. A sampling of our most notable alleged evildoers:

- The top one percent
- The top two percent
- Millionaires
- Billionaires
- Venture ("vulture") Capitalists
- Wall Street tycoons
- Hedge Fund managers
- Drug companies
- Oil industry lobbyists
- Corporate jet owners
- Chambers of commerce
- Insurance companies
- Fox News
- Walmart
- The Religious Right
- The National Rifle Association
- Americans for Prosperity

Come to think of it, anyone or anything that makes money, rejects political correctness, and tends to cling to their guns and religion (to borrow a phrase) is a potential foil for today's progressive class warriors, particularly in difficult economic times.

Soak The Rich

Of course, there is one over-arching problem presented by a class warfare-driven itinerary of tax increases aimed at the upper middle class and so-called "rich": even a 100 percent marginal tax would not produce the revenues necessary to jumpstart job creation in a depressed economy. Hence, the strange paradox behind the President's rhetorical campaign on behalf of a proposed Stimulus II in the summer and fall of 2011. On the one hand, there was limited expectation among the general public that income tax increases on the rich would create more jobs. This despite a new and serious push within the progressive intelligentsia to cite Clinton-era tax rates and economic growth in support of a "higher taxation / higher growth" mantra. Still, it is a difficult sell to expect the producer class to feel stimulated enough to generate new jobs as the result of an increased tax burden. Nevertheless, the rhetorical push for "fairness" and "equality" became increasingly aggressive as the anemic economic recovery continued to sputter. The President's prevailing notion was that a sustained class envy-inspired attack on the wealthy would cause the voting public to forget about the lack of new jobs produced by a prohibitively expensive, and by just about any measure unsuccessful, Stimulus. And, Obama was proven correct.

Another interesting aspect of the President's relentless campaign against wealth: it's as though the rich possess a nefarious capacity to escape their societal obligations. (Recall the Silicon Valley remarks.) The indictment proceeds along accusatory lines. "They" never seem to do the right thing, like pay up, pay up, and pay up. It is here that the hyper-progressive former community organizer truly emerges. And it is in front of far left audiences that the President typically tells us what he *really* thinks:

> ". . . [W]e need shared sacrifice. And that means ending
> the tax cuts for the wealthiest 2 percent of Americans in
> this country. We can afford it. (Applause.)

It's not because we want to punish success. It's because if we're going to ask everybody to sacrifice a little,
we can't just tell millionaires and billionaires they don't
have to do a thing—just relax, that's fine. We'll take care
of this. (Laughter.) Go count your money. That's fine.
(Laughter and applause.)

Because some of you bought my book, I fall in this
category. (Laughter.) I'm speaking about myself. I can
afford to do a little more, especially when the only way
to pay for these tax cuts for the wealthy is to ask seniors
to pay thousands of dollars more for health care . . . ."[8]

The President's flirtation with the so-called Buffet Rule is
similarly economically incoherent, but politically powerful. The
proposed legislation would impose a minimum 30 percent effective tax rate on millionaires, regardless of source of income. In
essence, this approach would eliminate the tax code's distinction
between capital gains and earned income. The alleged rationale:
"fairness" and "debt stabilization," but the numbers do not hold
up to scrutiny.[9] Columnist Charles Krauthammer beautifully
took on the incongruity of this approach:

> "Okay. Let's do the math. The Joint Committee on Taxa-
> tion estimates this new tax would yield between $4 billion
> and $5 billion a year. If we collect the Buffet tax for the next
> 250 years—a span longer than the life of this republic—it
> would not cover the Obama deficit *for 2011 alone.*"[10]

Krauthammer goes on to point out that such a proposal was
offered at a time when the US was suffering from a historically
weak recovery and had the highest corporate tax rate in the in-
dustrialized world.[11]

One additional and fascinating aspect of the class jealousy paradigm is the participation of super liberal, super wealthy individuals willing to denigrate their wealth and even their life's work in the interests of the progressive cause. Indeed, on the very same day the Obama campaign began its (ultimately successful) indictment of Mitt Romney's career at Bain Capital (and the field of private equity generally) the President was the guest of honor at a $35,800 a plate dinner hosted by Tony James, the president of private equity firm Blackstone.[12] But no better example presents itself than the case of billionaire investor Warren Buffett himself.

In 2012 Mr. Buffett famously bemoaned the fact that those who "make money with money" pay the lower capital gains rate on their income, as opposed to those who "earn money from a job." Now, millions of people are employed in one form of brokerage or another around the world. Most would offer that they use their brains, intellect, and judgment in order to make money for their clients and themselves. And that they work hard for their income. Yet, one of their most renowned, successful colleagues has quite an opposite opinion. *Forbes* contributor Richard Salsman captured the inconsistency best: "How odd that the world's most famous investor doesn't believe investing is a job."[13]

Odder still is the proliferation of mega wealthy market capitalists so eager to promote and fund politicians antagonistic to their businesses and employees. Many are entrepreneurial success stories (Bill Gates, Microsoft; Mark Zuckerberg, Facebook; Ted Turner, Turner Broadcasting; George Lucas, Hollywood director; Jim Sinegal, Costco; Mark Cuban, Dallas Mavericks) or hail from Wall Street (Jamie Dimon, JP Morgan Chase; Mark Gilbert, Barclays). That unabashed capitalist tycoons are some of the most generous contributors to America's progressive tide is irrefutable.

Alas, Economics 101 taught us how raising the capital gains tax impedes the free flow of capital. Such tax hikes encourage inefficiency in the capital markets. They do not contribute to wealth creation. They do not promote economic growth. But they sure sound attractive when uttered by charismatic class warriors who are themselves fabulously wealthy.

Leftist broadsides against success and wealth are nothing new. But for me, Obama era indictments of wealth and success brought back painful memories of a similar class gilded attack from the first Bush era. Who could forget the vitriol produced by the infamous "luxury tax" of 1990?

A Bad Idea

That oldie but goodie was included in the infamous budget reconciliation bill of that same year. It amounted to a 10 percent surcharge on certain luxury items: jewelry, furs, automobiles, and yachts. The proposed tax represented yet another attempt to ensure "fairness" in the midst of a budget crisis. It was applauded by left leaning pundits, and was accompanied by the now familiar class envy based rhetoric.[14] The usual static revenue analysis promised what the proponents of such measures always envision: lots more money into the federal treasury. The Joint Committee on Taxation estimated that new revenue would reach $31 million.[15] For the umpteenth time in economic history, a lack of dynamic analysis resulted in a wild overestimation of projected revenues. In essence, to the surprise of absolutely nobody outside of Washington, D.C., an increase in the cost of goods lowered marketplace demand for those same goods. An insightful piece by George F. Will captured the net economic damage inflicted by the new surcharge:

The tax destroyed 330 jobs in jewelry manufacturing, 1,470 in the aircraft industry and 7,600 in the boating industry. The job losses cost the government a total of $24.2 million in unemployment benefits and lost income tax revenues. So, the net effect of the taxes was a loss of $7.6 million in fiscal 1991, which means the government projection was off by $38.6 million . . . People bought yachts overseas. Who would have thought it?[16]

Numerous academic studies have been devoted to analyzing the damaging economic impact of this well publicized measure. Perhaps the most illuminating is a Heartland Institute blog post by Edmund Contoski:

> Within eight months after the change in the law took effect, Viking Yachts, the largest US yacht manufacturer, laid off 1,140 of its 1,400 employees and closed one of its two manufacturing plants. Before it was all over, Viking Yachts was down to 68 employees. In the first year, one-third of US yacht-building companies stopped production, and according to a report by the congressional Joint Economic Committee, the industry lost 7,600 jobs. When it was over, 25,000 workers had lost their jobs building yachts, and 75,000 more jobs were lost in companies that supplied yacht parts and material. Ocean Yachts trimmed its workforce from 350 to 50. Egg Harbor Yachts went from 200 employees to five and later filed for bankruptcy. The US, which had been a net exporter of yachts, became a net importer as US companies closed. Jobs shifted to companies in Europe and the Bahamas. The US Treasury collected zero revenue from the sales driven overseas.[17]

When it comes to special taxation directed to particular luxury items, there is yet another criticism properly lodged by opponents: arbitrariness and inconsistency. How else to characterize the wild fluctuations of Obama administration policy directed toward that favorite toy of the rich and famous, corporate jets?

Come Fly With Me

The early Obama administration waxed supportive of business investment proposals that benefited aircraft manufacturers. Such pronouncements are easily issued when the press is positive and the polls are high. For example, the federal tax bill that passed in December 2010 allowed companies to depreciate the cost of new equipment purchases over one year rather than a term of years. Luxury jet manufacturers celebrated the good news. It represented a positive move that went directly to their corporate bottom line. Yet, fast forward less than ten months and the same administration targets for elimination a long entrenched tax break for corporate jet owners.

A timely *Bloomberg* analysis further highlighted the administration's hypocrisy by pointing out that an Obama tour of an Alcoa plant in Bettendorf, Iowa in June of 2011 was intended to showcase the importance of the company's products to airplane manufacturers.[18] The president of the General Aviation Manufacturers Association summed up the administration's transparent inconsistency by stating, "he's [Obama] going after a segment of the aviation industry that uses Alcoa's products. We're just scratching our heads."[19]

Insightful political observers were not confused; pointed rhetorical strikes focused on income disparity and consumption of luxury items are *always* a safe refuge for progressive class warriors. And the vitriol is even more pronounced when the practitioner of the act has nothing to sell in the way of economic success. Indeed, one does not require a graduate degree in political science to understand the need to change the subject when record (sustained) unemployment, record deficits, record spending, and a record credit rating downgrade are one's economic . . . "record."

Alas, all is not lost, despite the tendency of Washington to simply ignore long term, intractable fiscal crises. But it took a historic election cycle and a loose confederation of grassroots protestors to pave the way toward historic reform. And herein lies yet another explanation for the left's anger and resentment: this Tea Party-inspired movement made a bit of progress in a way thought impossible at the very beginning of the Obama administration.

Tea Party Impact

So, how did the Tea Party reformers change the rules of engagement on Capitol Hill?

One needs to look no further than the debt limit deal of 2011 for tangible proof of the movement's clout within a revitalized House GOP caucus—and Washington's spending culture. Consider:

None of the good that came out of the 2011 budget showdown would have occurred but for the 2010 mid-term elections. Only a newly elected GOP House guaranteed that (at least some) deficit relief would be Priority One in the aftermath of two major Bush-era wars and profligate deficit spending during the Obama years. A Pelosi-led House would have simply rubber stamped the seventh debt limit increase over the previous three years with no questions asked by a compliant Congress.

Only a Republican House could *guarantee* no tax increases as part of a budget deal. An Obama-Reid-Pelosi leadership team would have done what it always does—included the termination of the Bush tax cuts as an essential element to any such plan. In the words of Ways & Means Committee Chairman Dave Camp, any proposed tax increase "[was] not going to happen."

Entitlement program cuts (Washington-speak for smaller increases) did not survive the budget machinations of 2011-12. But the aforementioned new House Members remain more than ready to commence heavy fiscal lifting. This determination to finally reform unchecked entitlement spending is not entirely new to Washington—there have been elements within both parties willing to engage in the past. What makes the present situation so historic is the number of Members (many elected in 2010) dedicated to doing what everyone knows needs to be done—future sophistic attack ads and fierce establishment criticism notwithstanding.

The 2011 deal was by no means a historic reordering of budget priorities. But rarely has a debt limit increase been linked to budget cuts in such a successful way. Further, in light of the strategy's success, this connection could become the new modus operandi for a conflicted Congress and executive branch. In effect, a feared spending paradigm (automatic budget cuts) has been created for bipartisan budget hawks forever on the hunt for new ways to control federal spending.

Alas, a limited budget deal did nothing to abate the fury with which the media elite have gone about the business of attacking the Tea Party and bemoaning the dysfunction in Washington. Simply put, leading liberal commentators have not been bashful regarding their utter frustration with those who simply will not be co-opted by the time-tested methodologies of the establishment. One notable observation about the Class of 2010: this crowd is not terribly intimidated when labeled "malcontents," "terrorists," "hostage takers," "Nazis," and more. This willingness to suffer the slings, arrows, and demonization campaigns of progressive activists is refreshing and a welcome change in Congressional culture. A further point: the philosophical gridlock that has transpired over the Obama years was predictable—even healthy. The American people sent wildly conflicting messages about what they want between the Obama-mania-election of 2008, the conservative revolution of 2010, and the status quo, divisive re-election campaign of 2012. The resulting clash between diametrically opposed world views should have been expected by everyone.

The Consequences of Bad Credit

The August 2011 credit rating downgrade of US debt served to strengthen the resolve of the young, hard charging fiscal hawks. Indeed, those ultra aggressive members who opposed the debt limit deal because it "didn't cut enough" were only empowered by Standard & Poor's historic edict that seemed to validate their strong concerns. Acting in unison, this determined new breed of budget hawk saw that a unified front provided them unbridled opportunity to effect real change in Congressional spending habits. Subsequent warnings about credit downgrades will further enable this hyper-aggressive group.

Change in this context meant using the ultimate budget sledgehammer: sequestration. This most blunt of budget instruments was the option of choice for makers of the grand compromise of 2011. The mere mention of the term sends Capitol Hill's big spenders into fits of moral outrage. In emotional tones they ask how anyone could adopt such an anti-intellectual approach to the needs of our citizenry. Indeed, sequestration is antithetical to the ways and means of the Capitol Hill process, wherein budget winners and losers are chosen as a function of which party is in power. In the land of sequestration, everybody and every agency is a loser, as the cuts are divided equally across the federal government. Here, percentage cuts do not distinguish between defense hawks and welfare advocates—all are simply given less money and told to do more with it. As such, sequestration follows in the grand tradition of congressional fast track authority, where sometimes irresponsible, non-accountable automatic results are produced precisely because Congress lacks the institutional discipline to make difficult decisions through its regular processes.

Yet in practice, even this allegedly draconian process has proven not to be immune from the time tested Capitol Hill practice of "earmarks," or in this case, "exemptions." One wrinkle, however, is that many of the special interests seeking such exemptions are forced to identify an appropriate set-off somewhere else in the federal budget—not an easy task as every special interest in Washington seeks to play defense in the strange, new era of sequestration politics.

The Other Side

In Washington, even successful movements have a downside, and Tea Party activism within the GOP is no exception. For example, there was decidedly mixed impact of Tea Party-sponsored candidates in key swing states during the 2010 midterm elections. Such impact was positive in Kentucky and Pennsylvania, where strong Tea Party-supported conservatives took relatively easy wins. The GOP win in Pennsylvania (Pat Toomey over Joe

Sestak) was particularly noteworthy, given that state's history of electing union-friendly Democrats.

The downside of Tea Party activism was equally present, however, as Democrat Chris Coons trounced Tea Party favorite Christine O'Donnell for an open seat in Delaware, and the extremely vulnerable Harry Reid survived a tight race over another Tea Party champion, Sharron Angle, in Nevada (wherein internecine battles wracked the anti-Reid forces). Many pundits observed that only untested candidates like O'Donnell and Angle could have lost such winnable races during a cycle wherein Republicans achieved historic mid-term gains.

In 2012 the continued demonization of all things Tea Party helped a decidedly vulnerable Democratic President win re-election. Again, despite no supportive evidence, a "racist" indictment was successfully lodged against Tea Party activists and Republican candidates, particularly in toss-up races. Only in this cycle the charges appear to have hit the mark with other critical swing groups: both Hispanics and Asians gave their votes to Obama by much higher margins than expected.[20]

Of course, such punditry fits well into the consistent mainstream media's narrative of dogmatic right wing zealots capturing the GOP base. The healthy dose of fiscal realism injected into the party by Tea Party activists contravenes this popular indictment, but missed Senate opportunities and Obama's re-election have slowed the Tea Party Express, at least in the short term.

Fiscal Education

Despite all the class envy-inspired platitudes produced by Washington's class warriors, Americans now have some familiarity with our recent fit of fiscal insanity. The evidence is quite revealing:

The federal deficit in February 2011 was equal to the entire deficit in 2007.

America's debt is more than 17 trillion dollars.

A visit to usdebtclock.org as of October 1, 2013 shows that the United States owes around $53,535 per citizen and more than $148,205 per taxpayer.

Fiscal year 2013 was the fifth consecutive year with a federal deficit exceeding $1 trillion.

Interest payments on the national debt is now the fifth largest item in the entire federal budget and projected to quadruple within 10 years, making it the second largest budget item behind Social Security and Medicare. Debt held by the public is roughly three-fourths the size of the entire economy; by the end of the decade, interest owed on the debt will be nearly $1 trillion.

According to the CBO, sometime around 2060 spending on Social Security, Medicare, and Medicaid alone will exceed the total of all federal revenues.[21]

These budget facts are mind numbing. And for the 99.9 percent of us who were not math majors, they are almost impossible to get one's brain around. But comprehend the arithmetic we must, as the deficit and what to do about it remain central to the future credit worthiness of the United States.

It's All About *Yes*

It is rather easy to understand how we ended up in this hole. It's all about the *politics of yes*—that persistent, bipartisan disease whereby presidents and legislators seek voter approval through limitless federal spending. Here, every new interest group (and spending request) is received approvingly. It's not difficult: just say "yes," tell the voters about your latest and greatest way to expand government, and cruise to re-election. Recent context is found in popular Democratic campaign ads from the 2012 election cycle. The familiar moral: hands off our sacrosanct entitlements—or else.

But both parties are at fault. Indeed, the guaranteed applause line is to point out that Republicans are the party of big government, while Democrats are the party of *really, really* big government. Consistent deficit spending over the past 30 years confirms this unfortunate laugh line.

It is an inconvenient truth (to borrow a phrase) that the politics of *yes* only works when the voters are complicit. On the left, there are precious few political or office holding consequences for overspending taxpayer dollars. The mindset is familiar enough: the fact of unmet societal needs requires additional spending to meet those needs. Again, check out the rhetoric from the Occupy crowd: *their* list of needs is endless, as are their expectations for government services and new revenue to fund those services.

The end of the Bush tax cuts? Sure, but not enough. The Buffett Rule? Sure, but not enough. Major new taxes on capital and consumption? Sure, but not enough.

This "not enough" drug is highly addictive; it can lead to denial about having a spending problem in the first place. Witness the President's revealing lament during testy fiscal cliff negotiations in December 2012. According to Speaker John Boehner, the President repeatedly cited escalating healthcare costs as the primary cause of the federal deficit, and insisted that "we don't have a spending problem." [22] The Speaker's persistent refrain about the ever-growing deficit finally led Obama to complain, "I'm getting tired of hearing you say that." [23] Instructive words that are reflective of an emboldened ideologue unwilling to confront the reality of Washington's insatiable desire to spend the people's money.

On the right, there is far too much situational conservatism. You know it when you see it: cut all those *other* programs, but just not mine. I had firsthand experience with this mindset as a Congressional Whip wherein "C-Span conservatives" (those Members who loved to rail against Washington spending in front of the cameras) would quietly and feverishly fight for their share of appropriations pork behind closed doors. It's not pleasant to watch, nor does it generate grassroots enthusiasm when exposed. *Everyone* has to be "all in" if we ever are to get serious about putting the brakes on our spending insanity.

Not so long ago it was incomprehensible that America's credit rating could be downgraded. Not too many years ago, persistent annual deficits in the trillions were poisonous to one's political ambitions. At the beginning of this millennium, it was never contemplated that one four-year term could add over $5 trillion to the national debt.

Yet, here we are with a re-elected Obama administration, staring down the barrel of yearly trillion dollar deficits and being lectured to *by the Chinese*.

A Ray of Hope

But all is not lost. True leaders recognize entitlement reform is the key ingredient in deficit reduction. And so it was in 2011 when two unlikely allies proposed a substantive plan to reform the most difficult entitlement, Medicare. Obamacare's impact on Medicaid is more thoroughly explored in a later chapter. For present purposes, let's just say this story is all about a rare willingness to step up and lead despite potentially dire political consequences.

Back then Congressman Paul Ryan was the not-so-widely-known Chairman of the House Budget Committee, while Ron Wyden was the reliably liberal junior Senator from Oregon. Yet both recognized Medicare was on an unsustainable fiscal path.

Accordingly, their reform plan allowed seniors to either stay enrolled in traditional Medicare or qualify for a government subsidy to help pay for private coverage.

That both took considerable political risk to lead on this third rail issue is an understatement. Ryan's vice presidential nominee performance earned him solid reviews, but his rising star is diminished every time a Democratic-sponsored "Mediscare" campaign succeeds. For Wyden, it's worse. Many Democratic partisans view him as a turncoat. Their lament: How can we claim Republicans want to throw granny over the cliff when one of our most prominent progressives is leading the charge for reform?

The Ryan-Wyden proposal was not perfect. But it was a substantial proposal. It deserves due consideration if we are finally serious about making progress in the battle against the politics of *yes*, the politics that leads to penny-wise and pound-foolish economic ruin.

The budget facts recited herein reflect a death spiral of monumental proportions. But they do constitute the predicate for a new breed of Washington politician intent on fiscal restoration. Further, the sheer magnitude of the numbers has transformed the national debt into a front burner, almost tangible, but politically improbable issue. In this respect, just imagine the positive budget implications if some form of the Ryan-Wyden proposal becomes law *and* the two principals survive and thrive politically.

The bottom line: real, albeit "minimal," spending cuts began pursuant to the 2011 debt ceiling deal and achieved more significant impact as sequestration hit home at the beginning of Obama II. And it does not matter if the cuts were achieved through a debt deal, a super-committee, or the regular appropriations process. They were accomplished, as the howls of protest from the political class will attest. Whether this initial step into fiscal reality leads to a successful budget "mega deal" (inclusive of entitlement reform) will play out over the second Obama administration.

The Way Forward

Deficit reduction will arrive (if at all) in a halting way during this new progressive era. A bitterly divided Congress and the re-election of Barack Obama have ensured this perilous road to progress.

Certainly recent history does not give one cause for much optimism. But we can hope. We can pray. We can protest. We can achieve cuts through periodic budget deals. We can make Harry Reid *minority leader* of the Senate. We *can* get it done, but it can only start with brutally honest plans and leaders willing to entertain great political risk.

| FISCAL SECURITY CHAPTER FOOTNOTES |

1. For an excellent analysis of the struggles attendant to maintaining a persuader's "agenda and spin," see: "The Only Authentic Book of Persuasion," Professor Richard E. Vatz, Towson University, Kendall Hunt Publishing Company, 2012.
2. Robin Bravender & Anna Palmer, "Wall Street Dems Can't Have it Both Ways," *Politico,* October 18, 2011.
3. Jennifer Liberto, "Wall Street set to break spending records this election," CNN Money, September 5, 2012.
4. Perhaps the most potentially devastating indictment lodged to this point has been the repeated charges of racism directed at the Tea Party

and its followers. The electrified allegation has now been repeated with enough frequency that it has stuck in the minds of some Americans—particularly African-Americans. See blue state African-American turn-out in 2010 and 2012 for corroborating evidence. This despite no evidence to corroborate the charge and an aggressive counter-attack waged by prominent black conservative leaders such as Herman Cain, Congressman Tim Scott, Congressman Allen West, and former Republican National Committee Chairman Michael Steele.

5. Jeff Mason, "Biden: U.S. needs more stimulus, business mad at S&P," http://www.reuters.com/article/2011/08/26/us-usa-biden-id USTRE77P46I20110826, *Reuters*, August 26, 2011.

6. Richard Cohen, "The President who Doesn't Care," *The Washington Post*, October 30, 2012.

7. Remarks by the President at a Facebook Town Hall, Facebook Headquarters, Palo Alto, California, http://www.whitehouse.gov/the-press office/2011/04/20/remarks-president-facebook-town-hall, April 20, 2011.

8. Remarks by the President at a DNC Fundraiser, Nob Hill Masonic Center, San Francisco, CA, April 21, 2011.

9. "The Obama Rule: He says taxation is about fairness, not growth or revenue," *The Wall Street Journal*, April 11, 2012; Joint Committee on Taxation Report JCX-73-12, Joint Committee on Taxation, September 19, 2012.

10. Charles Krauthammer, "The Buffett Rule: Free-Lunch Egalitarianism: Obama's disguised tax hike on capital gains," *National Review*, April 12, 2012.

11. Ibid.

12. Charles Riley, "Wall Street ditches Obama, backs Romney," CNN Money, May 29, 2012.

13. Richard Salsman, "Warren Buffett and Other Anti-rich Capitalists," *Forbes*, August 28, 2011.

14. Walter E. Williams, "Ignorance, Stupidity or Connivance?" Townhall.com, August 10, 2011.

15. Ibid.

16. George F. Will, "A Tax Break for the Yachting Class," *The Washington Post*, October 28, 1999.

17. Edmund Contoski, "Economically Illiterate Obama, re: Corporate Jets," *Heartland Institute blog,* July 12, 2011.
18. Richard Rubin and Andrew Zajac, "Corporate Jet Tax Gets Six Obama Mentions, $3 Billion Estimate," *Bloomberg* , June 30, 2011.
19. Ibid.
20. Presidential Exit Polling, *The New York Times*, http://elections.nytimes.com/2012/results/president/exit-polls
21. James Hammerton, "The Entitlement Deficit: America's Other National Debt," James Hammerton, June 3, 2011, freedomworks.org, and Patrick Louis Knudsen, "The Imperative of Spending Control," heritage.org, Patrick Louis Knudsen, October 12, 2011.
22. Kathryn Jean Lopez, "We Don't Have A Spending Problem," *National Review*, January 7, 2013.
23. Ibid.

AN INSECURE CULTURE

"To me the foundation of American life rests
upon the home and the family. I read into
these great economic forces, these intricate
and delicate relations of the government with
business and with our political and social life,
but one supreme end . . . that we strengthen the
security, the happiness, and the independence of
every home."

—HERBERT HOOVER

W e hear the phrase used all the time: "culture wars," a phrase originated in the public's mind from conservative commentator Patrick Buchanan's 1992 address to the Republican National Convention. A cottage industry of critical opinions devoted to one or another aspect of such wars has grown rapidly. Pundits and pols from the right and left seek constant engagement, often in very public ways. And there is no shortage of forums: daily, it's *The Times* vs. *The Journal*; Fox vs. MSNBC; Limbaugh vs. NPR; *The Nation* vs. *National Review*; The Heritage Foundation vs. The Center for American Progress. The passion is strong. Emotions run deep. The stakes are high indeed: an all out battle to define the contours and direction of American culture.

As each side desperately seeks the rhetorical high ground and the fights take on a fever pitch, it would serve everyone's interests to reach back for a timely lesson in American history. Maybe then a commonsense majority will assert its will, before it's too late.

Our historical refresher course begins with a familiar history of flight and freedom. It is a narrative that (not so long ago) was taught in every elementary school in America; a tale of horrific ocean voyages, hardscrabble lives, and self-sacrifice. The values have become romanticized over time, but nevertheless maintain their ageless relevance: religious tolerance, individual freedom, a common language, pluralism, democratic institutions, and market capitalism. God-given freedom was the common denominator. (It's what "inalienable rights" is all about.) Jointly, these values remain unique to the American experience, and remain instantly identifiable as foundational elements of our American culture.

So what's the problem? Why have essential elements of the American culture come under such vicious attack by the forces of liberalism, soon to be rhetorically mollified as progressivism, over the past few decades? Why has the educational establishment proven to be so acquiescent to revisionist impulses? And do these sustained attacks represent a serious threat to our cultural heritage as constructed over the past two hundred thirty seven years?

Initially, it is important to understand the full range of platforms available to the modern left. They range from the traditional (academia, public media, Hollywood, the arts) to the highly organized interest groups of the progressive movement (organized labor, gay rights, greenies, anti-war groups, feminists, and community advocates / organizers). These loosely affiliated groups and their common agendas are well-known and well-funded. Their reach into everyday life is deep and persistent. They influence major organs within the mass media and take maximum advantage of this access with regularity and seriousness. For present purposes, suffice to say each is heavily invested in bringing about fundamental changes to our culture from a decidedly left-leaning orientation.

It is obvious to even casual observers that cultural affronts perpetuated by the aforementioned groups are not going away anytime soon. Their determined campaigns are bankrolled by some of the wealthiest leftists in the world. As for the root cause(s) of the attacks, there are a multitude of motives to energize a political movement to undermine the foundational building blocks of a spectacularly successful culture. But that analysis must wait for another day, and another book. What I do understand is what the commonsense majority needs to do to defeat the progressive agenda. Accordingly, a number of important prescriptions are presented in the following pages.

An American Culture

Our analysis begins with the central issue of definition. More succinctly, the high stakes race to define the meaning of a singular American culture inclusive of individuals from different races and ethnicities. And to the winner will go a very big prize: how Americans view themselves (and how the world views America) in the new millennium.

At the outset, it is important to distinguish between the pluralism we so rightly celebrate and the multiculturalism we must reject. It is a distinction deliberately muddled by the progressive left. Accordingly, a pressing societal goal is presented to the general public in confusing ways. This confusion serves no good purpose and must be corrected at every turn. Fortunately, the remedy is easily identified: *re-establish the centrality of pluralism within a uniquely American culture*. Failure to do so allows for the consistent hijacking of a commonly understood term by a progressive movement keenly intent on remaking American culture in its own image.

For Americans, pluralism means the co-mingling of diverse ethnicities and races in one place. Our experience has shown this dynamic environment leads to the assimilation of diverse peoples into a singular culture where common values are taught, protected, and celebrated.

The American story is particularly poignant in this regard: most immigrants left their countries to escape religious persecution or seek economic opportunity. Some came to explore a new frontier. Kidnapped Africans arrived in leg irons aboard slave ships. Regardless of origin, almost all arrived in the new world with little or no money. What bound most of these disparate early arrivals together was an expectation (although not immediately available to all) that freedom and opportunity awaited them; that economic mobility could be achieved through hard work; that religious tolerance would be embraced; that no king or monarch would ever rule over them; and that the rule of law would reign supreme, blind to one's formal education, economic status, or bloodlines.

In return, the people agreed to recognize the laws, language, and (emerging) customs of the new nation. This general recognition became the societal denominator; a commonality of interests emerged including religious tolerance, market capitalism, personal freedoms, baseball, and apple pie. A uniquely American culture was born, and grew into the most successful democratic enterprise the world has ever seen.

This brief but telling history lesson is deeply familiar to the average American. It is retold every Fourth of July. It is the story of a wildly successful experiment into common values, assimilation, and freedom. It is what continues to draw the oppressed and downtrodden from all over the planet. Most importantly, it continues to be accepted (and celebrated) by a clear majority of our citizens. But it is a source of great irritation to various malcontents on the left who wish to remake our culture, and our self image. They wish to do so because so many reject the notion of the grand experiment itself; the American melting pot is not *their* goal. Indeed, they vilify the founding fathers. They see America as the product of cultural cleansing and forced assimilation. They cultivate victims and demand governmental apologies (and reparations) for territorial and cultural aspirations. In some cases, they wish to claim (or reclaim) independent status—independence from our Judeo-Christian heritage and American culture. And failing such lofty goals, they seek to create a truly multicultural society, where melting pots are assailed and separatism is celebrated.

Fortunately, the forces of multi-cultural progressivism have lately been forced on the defensive. Culture warriors representing the commonsense majority have made real progress, especially as the growth of Islamist extremism has required political leaders to acknowledge what had recently been regarded as a (cultural) third rail: governmentally enforced multiculturalism is a dangerous failure.

A Change of Attitude

Surprisingly, heretofore politically correct European democracies have not proven immune from the refreshing change of attitude. In February 2011, British Prime Minister David Cameron observed "multiculturalism is dead," thereby echoing similar views expressed by German Chancellor Angela Merkel in 2010.[1] In doing so, Cameron joined a growing chorus of western leaders willing to stand up to the multicultural apologists who have preached (and practiced) separatism within the oldest pluralistic democracies the world has seen. It is clear the rise of radical Islam sped up the British disdain for the anti-assimilation crowd,[2] but it was inevitable that such social separatism would fail: it can only be a brief period of time wherein disparate ethnicities can co-exist (let alone prosper) without the emergence of common bonds and a commonality of interests. A wonderfully written *Wall Street Journal* opinion piece by Douglas Murray (reviewing a speech by Prime Minister Cameron) captures the growing English frustration and newfound willingness to engage (and defeat) multicultural apologists from the left:

> Finally, Europe's mainstream party leaders seem to be realizing what others have long noticed: Multiculturalism has been the most pernicious and divisive policy pursued by Western governments since World War II . . . .
>
> The multicultural model may have continued a lot longer if it hadn't been for radical Islam. The terrorist assaults and plots across Britain and Europe—often from home-grown extremists—provided a breaking point that few sentient people could ignore. The question now is what can be done.
>
> In his speech in Munich, Mr. Cameron rightly focused on the problem of home-grown Islamic extremism. He stressed several preliminary steps—among them that groups whose values are opposed to those of the state will no longer be bestowed with taxpayer money. It is a symptom of how low we have sunk that ceasing to fund our societies' opponents would constitute an improvement.
>
> But this is a first, not a final, policy. The fact is that Britain, Germany, Holland and many other European countries have nurtured more than one generation of citizens who seem to feel no loyalty toward their country and who, on the contrary, often seem to despise it.

The first step forward is that from school-age upward our societies must reassert a shared national narrative—including a common national culture. Some years ago the German Muslim writer Bassam Tibi coined the term "Leitkultur"—core culture—to describe this. It is the most decent and properly liberal antidote to multiculturalism. It concedes that in societies that have had high immigration there are all sorts of different cultures—which will only work together if they are united by a common theme.[3]

It was only a few years prior to Cameron's comments that a Pew poll found a shocking 81% of British Muslims saw themselves as Muslims first and a citizen of their country second.[4] But it was another conservative leader who struck a brutally frank chord of opposition early in the new millennium. The year was 2006, the leader was Australian Prime Minister John Howard, and the words were (and remain) remarkably instructive:

Australia has been greatly enriched by immigration and most people who have come to this nation have happily integrated with the community.

They have willingly embraced the Australian way of life. They have become part of the fabric of the nation and have helped make Australia the great country it is today.

I have said many times that people who come to this country —no matter where they are from—should become part of the Australian community.

For new migrants, that means embracing Australian values, accepting our culture, being able to speak English if it's not their first language and understanding that men and women have equality.

But it is an undeniable fact that some who have come here are resisting integration. There are pockets of this resistance in different migrant groups but it is perhaps most visible at this time in a small section of the Islamic community.

A small minority of this community, and other groups that reject integration, regard appeals for them to fully integrate into the Australian way of life as some kind of discrimination.

It is not. It is common sense and, importantly, it is also a powerful symbol of a new migrant's willingness and enthusiasm about becoming an Australian.

It is difficult to get anywhere in this country without learning English. It's the common language of Australia and is, quite simply, a passport to the future.

Simple tasks like securing a job and making new friends would be so much harder in Australia without a working knowledge of English.

Treating women as equals is an Australian value that should be embraced. Australians generally do not tolerate women being treated in an inferior fashion to men...

We are an egalitarian nation that prides itself on the concept of a fair go, our equal treatment of men and women, our parliamentary democracy, and free speech.

Embracing these values and other Australian ideals is vital for new arrivals. All new arrivals.

But it is self-evident that some people are resistant to Australian values. There are small sections of some communities, including the Islamic community, that are resistant to integration.

As I have said on many occasions, 99 percent of the Islamic community of Australia has integrated into, and is part of, the Australian community. They have added great value to our society and are making a valuable contribution to the nation . . .

Perhaps we can take a lead from the pupils of Eastwood Heights Public School, a school in Sydney's northwest that I visited yesterday. The students share family backgrounds from all corners of the world. But it was immediately obvious they have quickly learned the values of tolerance, respect, fairness and equality. A vibrant example for all Australians.[5]

Unsurprisingly, the response from progressive pols and their media allies to this wonderfully crafted statement was disapproving and emotional. The always expected and typically over the top charges of racism and xenophobia rang out from all the usual corners, but they had no legs.[6] The Prime Minister successfully fortified his commonsense views during a subsequent media frenzy. This willingness to stand up to the easily insulted left is an important personality trait for today's conservative leader—a point more fully explored in Chapter 4 of *Turn This Car Around*.

Never Ending Battles

Any celebration to the effect that this dangerous concept has been de-fanged should be placed on hold, however. These and other commonsense pronouncements about the importance of common values across diverse cultures and ethnicities are generally provided by right wing leaders and right wing media to the approval of right wing audiences. Presently, we have yet to see any prominent progressive reject the central thrust of multiculturalism. Should a progressive (or any left-of-center leader for that matter) arrive at a similar conclusion, however, it *would* be cause for celebration. Unfortunately, the commonsense majority has no reason to believe that such an admission may be forthcoming in the short run. Accordingly, we must understand that practitioners of the claim will not give up without a monumental fight.

Our future tactics in this regard are clear: continue to engage; continue to expose the emptiness of the agenda; and continue to carry the day in the eyes of the general public.

This last point deserves further emphasis precisely because the incremental defeat of the tarnished concept is not easily accomplished. Progressive interest groups have too much invested in a far-reaching guilt trip narrative to simply retreat or go away; they are "all in" when it comes to the gospel of multiculturalism. They are in business to degrade the concept of a singular American culture. They are determined to maintain identity politics—it is their lifeblood. They understand that their ability to propagate an aggressive separatism is wholly reliant on the race and ethnicity card(s). It is the number one tool in the multicultural playbook, and a proven winner with the mainstream media.

The Business of Race

The growth of racial identity politics since the advent of the civil rights movement has been analyzed from right and left. That this growth industry has manifested itself solely within the Democratic Party is readily apparent; Democratic candidates (regardless of race) regularly receive 9 out of 10 African American votes. Explanations for this consistent voting pattern are regularly offered up by intellectuals and pundits alike, including yours truly in my first book, *Turn this Car Around*.

But it is a subset of race politics that is most germaine to our critique of American culture: the peculiar notion that African American success, academic achievement, and wealth are somehow antithetical to black culture.

One of the most noxious manifestations of this narrative holds that academic achievement is "white," i.e., not to be emulated. An array of successful African American leaders from Martin Luther King, Jr. to Bill Cosby to the Reverend Jesse Jackson have sought to degrade the concept, but with some pushback from adherents. Fortunately, such a counter-productive worldview remains a minority position, but not *enough* of a minority view for comfort. To make matters worse, a related symptom of the disease emerges from time to time in the form of black-on-black stereotyping. High profile, conservative African-Americans are all too familiar with the indictment. Ask Condoleezza Rice, Clarence Thomas, Thomas Sewell, Walter Williams, J.C. Watts, or any number of well-known black Republicans how they are regularly dismissed / insulted by the purveyors of racial identity politics.

Think such racial profiling is confined to right leaning politically active blacks? Think again. Even hugely popular African Americans are not immune to the treatment. Witness the following dialogue from sports writer Rob Parker on ESPN's popular show, "First Take" [Regarding Washington Redskins quarterback Robert Griffin III]:

> My question, which is just a straight honest question: Is he a brother, or is he a cornball brother? . . . He's black, he kind of does his thing, but he's not really down with the cause, he's not one of us . . . I want to find out about him. I don't know because I keep hearing these things. We all know he has a white fiancée. Then there was all this talk about he's a Republican, which there's no information at all . . . "

Apparently, "us" is to view with great suspicion a young man who graduated from Baylor in three years, respects his parents, won the Heisman Trophy, generates one of the highest selling jerseys in the NFL, treats fans and reporters with patience and respect, and is the hottest commercial pitch man in professional sports because . . . he is married to a white woman and might (gasp!) carry a Republican voting card. "Us" should be shamed into submission because it wishes to follow a counter-cultural path so corrosive to American culture. Post script: Parker was suspended for 30 days by ESPN but should not have been penalized for his remarks. He was offering a critique that is widespread (if not deep) and should be heard, the better to take it down at every opportunity.

The race and ethnicity portion of our analysis is easily understood: it's all about assimilation—a concept under increasing assault from the cultural left, but one that must remain an essential element of what it means to be (and live like) an American.

A Values Society

The flipside is more complicated, but equally important. It's about the *values* that undergird the culture. Whose values? Are they malleable? Should they evolve over time? How flexible should majoritarian values be in a pluralistic society?

The list of "ageless" values cited at the beginning of this chapter is not exhaustive, but constitutes a good place to start the discussion. Religious tolerance, individual freedom, a common language, pluralism, democratic institutions, and market capitalism spell A-M-E-R-I-C-A. Presently, each of these fundamental values is undergoing a serious challenge engineered by a rabidly aggressive progressive movement only further encouraged by the re-election of President Obama. These challenges are not necessarily related, but have a similar purpose: effectuate fundamental change to the agreed-upon cultural value system adopted by a clear majority of American citizens for more than 200 years. The challenges are in many cases fierce, but facts and common sense must prevail if we are to carry the day.

So how vicious have the progressive attacks become? How far out of bounds (and out of common sense) have the ultrasensitive progressives been willing to go in the interest of challenging (and replacing) our cultural values? The answer to both inquiries is plenty; plenty vicious and plenty over the line when attempting to degrade our value system. For those not paying attention or who remain unconvinced, herewith a brief sampling of progressive shots taken from recent news accounts, for your consideration.

Christmas and Our Judeo-Christian Heritage

Post-2012 election polls reflect an increasingly secular America. Attendance at weekly religious services continues to decline. And the secularist/atheist campaign against religion in American life proceeds unabated. For example, there is a never-ending list of media reports about the latest upset to the American secularist's self-proclaimed right to be free of any and all religious influence. The stories multiply around Christmas, for obvious reasons. Two of recent vintage, however, stick out as representative of much that's wrong with the counter-cultural campaign against Christmas observances and celebrations.

- For 50 years, a Christmas tree and crèche were the only Christmas displays at the Loudoun County, Virginia courthouse. In recent years, however, the scenery has undergone dramatic change, as atheist testimonials, a skeleton Santa Claus mounted on a cross, and a mocking Nativity scene (sans Jesus) built by the "Church of the Flying Spaghetti Monster" are provided equal billing on the courthouse lawn.[7] As noted above, such anecdotes are no longer new: atheists and secular progressives have made similar stands (with varying degrees of success) over the past three decades. The ferocity of these incidents has led leading conservative media outlets, particularly Fox News, to not only "adopt" Christmas, but also to commence a counter-offensive against all combatants who have declared war on the Christian character of Christmas.

- An Arkansas atheist group successfully blocked the scheduled field trip of a Little Rock elementary school to a matinee production of a "Charlie Brown Christmas" at a local church. Seems the "Arkansas Society of Free Thinkers" saw Charlie, Lucy, and the gang as a threat to church/state separation. The most serious danger: Linus' reading of scripture devoted to the birth of Jesus Christ; what Christmas is really all about. Unhappily, the church's pastor decided to forego what promised to be an expensive court battle by canceling the show.8 Who said we always win 'em in the Bible Belt?

On the lighter side, cultural warriors are correct to oppose the slow, but steady replacement of "Merry Christmas" with "Happy Holidays" as the dominant holiday season greeting. This empty phrase is intended to cover all mid-winter holidays, sort of a blanket greeting for the winter solstice, with no particular religion or sect provided special treatment. This emptiness ensures that nobody could possibly be offended by the words, except Christians and traditionalists, of course, two distinctly unimportant audiences to the culturally correct. As such, it is politically correct-speak taken to its illogical extreme.

How much ground has been lost on this most familiar of greetings? Well, so much that the wise men and women of the Texas legislature saw fit to pass a "Merry Christmas Bill" in the spring of 2013.[9] The controversial bill seeks to do all types of radical things, such as allowing public school teachers to say "Merry Christmas" while on public school property. The notion of which set various Texas-based atheist groups off on their familiar mantra of "separation of church and state." Fortunately, Governor Rick Perry had the good sense to sign the bill. Religious liberty lives in The Lone Star State.

A Constitutional Reality Check

What to do: a reinvigorated commonsense majority must revisit (in order to teach) fundamental truths about religious practice in America. A good place to begin would be an historically accurate rejoinder to the false dichotomy between church and state: the framers never used the phrase, nor bought into the notion that religion had no place in the establishment of American ideals and institutions.[10] From its infancy, the country was about religious freedom and tolerance; never about separating ourselves from our religious heritage. For those in denial about this readily apparent truth, please check out the back of a penny, or listen to the way Congress begins its daily business, or think about why our military services employ ordained chaplains. Even the most difficult to reach should be able to figure it out from there. In this same vein, it is important to note that neither the framers nor the courts have guaranteed an individual's right to live in an offense-less society. To wit, the dominant culture has a right to observe its traditions and customs, even where such observances may cause someone or something to take offense. This view may be antithetical to the progressive crowd, but it remains common sense to the commonsense majority. As for the growing popularity of generic greetings at Christmas time, there is one remedy: just say it; do it; forget the ACLU and the hopelessly sensitive; be unapologetic about it—let rip as many "Merry Christmas-es" as possible—even if you don't live in Texas. You will feel better for your courage!

Income Disparity and Free Market Capitalism

Some on the far left (and more intermediate venues) point to household debt reaching 90% of GDP in support of a proposal to discharge all individuals and households within the so-called bottom 99% from any and all of their financial obligations to any institution that accepted federal aid as a result of the banking implosion of 2008-2009. The concept is derived from the Old Testament concept of "Jubilee"—a wholesale forgiveness of private debts. Today, a more modern rationale is offered: the newly debt-relieved masses will go on a massive spending spree which would in turn spark a long overdue economic recovery. According to the proponents, any impact on our banking and credit systems would be minimal, and who cares about all those greedy bankers anyway?[11] After all, they're the ones who got us into this horrific fiscal mess in the first place, right? One lefty blogger offered support for this proposal with a familiar egalitarian perspective: "For a nation that's forgiven economy decimators, Gulf of Mexico destroyers, torturers, and pointless-war starters, debt forgiveness simply seems like a logical next step."[12]

What to do? Hopefully, not much. We can hope this particularly goofy Occupy-induced idea stays dead. The proposal would undermine the most vital element of our economy: credit worthiness. Indeed, the most serious consequence of the mortgage crisis was the dramatic contraction of credit and its impact on consumers and businesses. Five years later, businesses remain on a tepid track to recovery and consumers remain hesitant to spend even after historic market intrusions by the Federal Reserve and Congress (read "TARP" and "Quantitative Easing I & II") helped keep a shaky banking system (and economy) from collapse.

On Marriage and Family

As the second decade of the new millennium began, headlines blared the news from the nation's leading media outlets: for the first time in American history, married couples are no longer the majoritarian family unit.[13] The reactions from all sides of the culture wars were predictable. Progressives conveyed their approval, conservative family groups their disapproval, and the story remained big national news for...a day. Such is the nature of issue priorities during the latter stages of a weak economic recovery that followed one of the deepest recessions in U.S. history. But the reaction (or lack thereof) also spoke to recent successes enjoyed by progressive cultural value makers who have been challenging the traditional family (and, more recently, traditional marriage) for years.

The Supreme Court's Defense of Marriage Act (DOMA) decision (in June of 2013) to pass on whether gay marriage is a Constitutional right means that the issue will play out in state legislatures and on state referenda for the foreseeable future. As both sides dig in for the long haul, the respective arguments pro and con have become familiar enough. But proponents would do well to ratchet back the demonizing of the opposition. Many opponents of gay marriage are neither homophobic nor religious zealots. In fact, some in the public sector endured harsh criticism from the right (yours truly included) when appointing gay Marylanders to judgeships and other senior positions in government or creating medical and custodial accommodations for non-traditional relationships—so vitriol from the left is not so intimidating.

Supporters now have adopted a "marriage equality" moniker and a civil rights narrative. Here, the inability to marry a person of the same sex is analogized to a Jim Crow-brand of discrimination. In the same way Rosa Parks was denied her civil right to sit wherever she wished on that city bus, supporters of gay marriage advance a similar right to marry a person of the same sex. And, take note: this argument has gained tremendous momentum in the courts and within our culture over the past ten years.

That America has made significant progress in combatting discrimination against gays is a fact. Anti-gay hazing, bullying, and violence has generated national attention and advanced a national dialogue. (Indeed, with regard to crimes committed against gays, I signed a bill that added sexual orientation as a protected class under Maryland criminal law.) Further, most Americans continue to see a limited role for government within the confines of one's bedroom. This newly energized libertarian spirit is most especially alive and well on college campuses and within a younger generation, a majority of whom have become supporters of gay marriage.

Many of us continue to draw the line at traditional marriage, however. It is integral to our Judeo-Christian heritage. So, we ask the state to defend this fundamentally important (albeit flawed) institution—not redefine it. A further point: supporters of traditional marriage must recognize that non-traditional relationships can and do produce loving environments and successful children. But children raised without dual gender parents continue to face unique obstacles. The professional literature in this respect is clear and serious leaders from the left and right once recognized this, including prominent Democratic Senator Daniel Patrick Moynihan more than forty years ago.

Divorce and Fatherlessness

A related cultural fault line is the very serious issue of divorce and its negative impact on children. A popular progressive indictment of traditional marriage cites a persistently high divorce rate. The argument proceeds as to why so much energy should be directed toward respecting and defending a flawed institution. Why try to fix something that breaks about 50% of the time? Again, the answer should be self-evident: human frailties do not negate the primary marital mission—child rearing—a job significantly and reliably more effectively accomplished through the presence of two parents.

Indeed, the epidemic of father-absent homes has had significant negative impact on our country and culture. The supporting sociological and economic data speaks to a cultural catastrophe:

- Children in father-absent homes are five times more likely to be poor. The poverty rate for single mother families (in 2011) was 40.9%, almost five times more than the rate of 8.8% for married couple families.[14]
- Fatherless children are twice as likely to drop out of school.[15]
- Young men who grow up in homes without fathers are twice as likely to end up in jail as those who come from

traditional two-parent families...those boys whose fathers were absent from the household had double the odds of being incarcerated—even when other factors such as race, income, parent education and urban residence were held constant. [16]

- 63% of youth suicides are from fatherless homes.[17]
- 85% of all children that exhibit behavioral disorders come from fatherless homes.[18]

Epidemics typically generate an emotional response from the afflicted, especially where the disease brings about great carnage. Yet, one of the most gruesome conditions within contemporary America proceeds apace, with only periodic bursts of serious attention.

It should not be lost on policy makers (and taxpayers) that all of the traditional markers (homelessness, runaways, dropouts, single female heads of household) have direct links to poverty. They also have direct links to increased public costs through government assistance programs.

Of course, not all fatherless homes suffer impoverishment or produce troubled children. There are many hard working single parents and guardians who overcome daunting obstacles to raise highly successful children. Often, grandparents, extended family, mentors, and friends help in filling the void left by an absent dad. But cases of beating the odds are more the exception than the rule; fatherlessness continues to be an accurate predictor of adolescent dysfunction.

The mere citation of the foregoing numbers can rile certain progressive pundits into hyper-defensive mode, as if the recognition of the problem and its awful consequences is somehow "insensitive." The time for sensitivity has come and gone. A politically correct lens will not hide the damage brought about by this phenomenon. And time is of the essence. Every day without a renewed culture-wide commitment to active fatherhood means more kids placed at risk; every day produces more kids headed for a criminal justice system ill equipped to handle the myriad mental health problems typically carried by this troubled population.

Lost Children

During my tenures as governor, congressman, and state legislator, I was a regular visitor to Maryland's juvenile and adult correctional facilities. Often, I left in a melancholy mood. These are no places for the faint of heart. The scenes are right out of "Scared Straight," and disturbingly predictable: jails full of mostly young men with little formal education. Gang affiliations are common. Dropouts are plentiful. Many are alcohol or substance abusers. Some suffer from mental illness. Few possess marketable skills. And a majority comes from fatherless homes.

Yet, our correctional system is expected to perform rehabilitative miracles. But far too many of our young offenders are received in damaged condition. Resources are limited and turnarounds are difficult (but not impossible) to achieve. And the task is made ever more challenging by the absence of an involved father.

A Coach's Perspective

Personal experience has further strengthened my views as to the pivotal role of fathers and male role models in childhood development. I have coached a youth football team for the last seven years. (Yes, there are advantages to life in the private sector.) This experience has allowed me to observe firsthand the physical and emotional development of young boys from a variety of racial, ethnic, and economic backgrounds. My (reinforced) takeaway should be familiar to the vast majority of readers: boys *crave* father-inspired discipline (and approval), especially in their formative years.

In life, as in politics, it's dangerous to generalize; there are always exceptions to any rule. Nevertheless, observation has shown me how boys who lack a male authority figure typically suffer from lack of discipline, concentration, and appreciation for authority. The all-important trust factor is absent in many such cases. Boys need men to instruct and guide them, *particularly* as progressivism seeks to de-masculinize the culture. In fact, in those situations where the trust deficit is present, a teacher-coach often morphs into the (revered) male authority figure. For those male athletes fortunate enough to gain such a mentor, it can be a transformational event that carries through high school and college.[19]

The Importance of Dads

So many social issues tend to break along liberal and conservative lines. This issue, however, stands alone. A forty year downturn in father-present families has inflicted great damage on our culture. Young children require parental guidance, and fathers play an essential role in providing it. Despite periodic delusional messages from Hollywood to the contrary, this notion still represents a majoritarian view. And everyone from President Obama to Jay-Z to Newt Gingrich has said so.

Nevertheless, too much lip service and not enough actual fatherhood has produced too many problematic young people. Our cultural epidemic of fatherlessness is out of control. It reflects a weakening of our cultural values. And there is no one government program to save the day, either. It must be a collective effort to fix our culture, to make such results unacceptable in America. Failure to act will perpetuate our present desultory track, a truly unacceptable result.

Rampant Illegitimacy

Another time bomb eats away at contemporary culture: illegitimacy.

It's not so politically correct to discuss the issue these days, and that's part of the problem. We should (must) talk about what everyone from our foremost social scientists to the man on the street *know* to be true: many out-of-wedlock babies carry an express ticket to the welfare rolls.

Illegitimacy rates have exploded since the 1960s. Today, 29% of white babies, 53% of Hispanic babies, and 73% of African-American babies are born illegitimate. And 71% of all illegitimate babies are born into poverty. The conservative commentator, Patrick J. Buchanan, described these statistics as reflecting a "headlong descent into social decomposition."[20] It is difficult to argue with Mr. Buchanan's analysis.

What to do? First, continue to resist the progressive campaign against the traditional family. And beware the resulting name calling: defenders are regularly dismissed as Neanderthal, extreme, or—the cruelest cut of all: un-cool. A not-so-recent case-in-point: Vice President Dan Quayle was nationally roasted for criticizing the fictive single TV mom Murphy Brown. Here, the Hollywood values makers were able to drive a cultural dagger into the heart of traditional marriage *and* make their point about the single woman's "right to choose" the lifestyle of her choice. To these points, a firm response is required: judgment may be un-cool, it may generate criticism from the mainstream media, but it is required if we are to sustain our cultural value system—a value system that recognizes most real-life Murphy Browns sentence their single head of household families to poverty. Census (poverty) data tells the unsurprising story. Married white couples have a poverty rate of 3.2%; the rate for their unmarried counterparts is 22%. The same spike applies to African Americans (7.0% to 35.6%) and Hispanics (13.2% to 37.9%).[21] Striking numbers indeed, but somehow acceptable for the "anything goes" crowd.

The required course of action is simple: a commonsense majority must not be afraid to exercise (and trumpet) sound judgment as to the cultural values it wishes to protect—ugly name calling from the opposition notwithstanding.

English

"This amendment is racist. I think it's directed basically to people who speak Spanish," exclaimed Senate Majority Leader Harry Reid on the Floor of the United States Senate on May 17, 2006.[22] The amendment that so exercised Reid would have made English the official language of the United States. Fortunately, Reid's comment had no impact; the full Senate approved the measure by a wide margin. Shortly thereafter, the seriousness of the proponents shone again as a second amendment, this one declaring English the "common and unifying language," passed by an overwhelming majority.[23]

The notion that English should be our official language reflects a majoritarian view; poll after poll finds a clear majority of Americans in support.[24] Interestingly, the same polls reject the claim that requiring people to speak English is a form of racism, an opinion shared by a majority of Hispanics.[25] A clear and consistent pattern emerges from the data: Americans of all racial and ethnic backgrounds believe immigrants have an *obligation* to adopt American culture, particularly its language.

Unfortunately, mean-spirited indictments from the likes of Harry Reid and like-minded progressives are the "go to" rejoinders whenever a foundational tenet of American culture is at issue. A familiar secondary charge implies that a defense of English translates into a disapproval of bilingualism. In response, commonsense culture warriors must distinguish between the need for a common language and the advantages of bilingualism. The former is a necessity if immigrants are to experience economic prosperity and assimilation; the latter is increasingly important as a way for adults to maximize their economic potential in an era of international trade and multi-national employers. This distinction is not complex, but must be properly communicated in the face of an often hostile mainstream media.

A Broken Immigration Policy

Sounds great, but how can we celebrate our cultural values and assimilation when our immigration system is *so* broken? And so it is here, at the intersection of culture and immigration policy, where the right finds itself on the defensive in its continuing battle with progressivism. Here, an aggressive defense of our cultural values often leads to charges of racism, or nativism, or ethnocentrism—the go-to "isms" so popular with the politically correct police. Of course, this insensitivity indictment misses the real point: a flourishing culture is dependent on sound immigration policy. It brings new talent and rich texture to the people, so long as newly arrived immigrants are willing to buy into their new culture.

This last point is where progressives lose the moral high ground. Their advocacy or, at least, acquiescence on behalf of open borders, lax immigration enforcement, and multiculturalism is a tripling down on bad policy. It degrades the legal system and culture. And it needs to be called out at every opportunity, before defenders of the rule of law are made secondary actors within our long-running immigration debate.

How To Fix It

But what are the elements of a positive immigration agenda? First, we should chastise both political parties for their benign neglect. A porous southern border is a long-running fact of life, and neither Republican nor Democratic administrations have done much to correct the situation. For Republicans, this inattention is (at least in part) attributable to a fear of offending Hispanic voters, an increasingly reliable Democratic voting block that made a real difference for Barack Obama in 2012. A deeper indictment rests on the realization that this indifference is manifested in a post 9/11 world. A mere twelve years later and border enforcement is a second-tier issue. How quickly we forget!

Second, it is important to re-engage legal immigration advocates. These groups own the moral high ground. *They* did the right thing, often waiting years to secure their citizenship. *They* are the silent majority who has special standing in the national debate. They must keep their priority status as comprehensive reform unfolds.

With regard to enforcement policy, real border security must be "Priority One." A functional fence,[26] adequate manpower, appropriate surveillance and detention assets, and an objective way to measure results represent the minimum commitment required of any national administration. As the seeds of a comprehensive agreement begin to grow, a degree of bipartisan consensus has emerged around the need to secure the border first.

Illegal aliens already here present a practical challenge. Members of the commonsense majority want our immigration laws enforced. They believe violations of such laws require sanctions. And this is where reality bumps into the rule of law. For example, no serious person has described how eleven million people (or more) could be rounded up and subjected to mass deportation. Family disruption would be massive, and hurtful. Manpower needs and associated logistics would be cost prohibitive. This grand plan may appeal to the anti-immigrant instincts of some, but it fails the reality test.

Contemporary Washington does not lack for immigration reform plans, including proposals pushed by the likes of Senator Marco Rubio and the so-called bipartisan "Gang of Eight." And one of the more sound approaches advocated by these leaders, among others, is to institute a transparent process whereby illegals who have lived here for many years, worked, paid income taxes, and possess health insurance are presented with a chance to obtain legal status and, potentially, residence and citizenship.[27]

In the interest of fundamental fairness (in addition to the bare minimum necessary to secure GOP/conservative support), these so-called probationary applicants would be subjected to a thorough criminal background check, required to be current on any taxes owed the government, required to learn English, show a work history, and prove current employment in the U.S. Upon successful completion of these items, this group would then be placed in line *behind* those who followed the law in requesting green card status. Note that the successful completion of the process only earns an opportunity to apply for the card.

There are numerous reform proposals in the works, but the foregoing elements are (1.) common to many plans, and (2.) politically viable. The advantages are evident: people are properly counted, a legitimate green card/guest worker program is empowered, additional tax revenue is collected, an illegal act is *not* rewarded with (an automatic) path to citizenship, the ill-conceived step of requiring applicants to first return to their native country prior to beginning the process is eliminated, and respect for the rule of law is (hopefully) renewed.

Of course, a successful program requires easily accessible nationwide employer verification. Fortunately, the required technology exists: the E-Verify system first introduced in 2007 is increasingly accurate and popular with employers. This system allows employers to check prospective employee personal information against Social Security Administration and Homeland Security databases, thereby confirming or rejecting a proposed employee's legal status. The program has been refined to where it is now more than 99% accurate at identifying those who are eligible for lawful employment in the U.S.

Accordingly, it should not be political heavy lifting to pass meaningful sanctions for those employers who nullify or mishandle the program. The bottom line is the required technology exists and should be utilized. And heretofore negligent employers beware: it's about time everyone got on board with this program.

The States

The bipartisan failure of the federal government to involve itself in serious immigration reform has left a number of divisive immigration issues to the states. Among these, funding for advocate groups supportive of illegal immigration, in-state college tuition for the children of illegal aliens, and driver's licenses for undocumented individuals are the most topical, and important.

So, what's a governor to do about all this? The answer is "plenty" when the federal government chooses to ignore its job.

In Arizona, a Republican governor and legislature famously passed its own immigration reform that gave local law enforcement (alleged) extra-constitutional authority to inquire into the immigration status of detainees. The well-reported statute made its way to the Supreme Court, where the most controversial aspect of the law (law enforcement's ability to check into the immigration status of a legally detained suspect) was upheld. A lesser known initiative from the Arizona legislature had the state collecting donations from the public to help finance a fence along the state's entire border with Mexico. Approximately $250,000 was raised during the project's first four months.[28] Those actions have provoked much progressive outrage, but also plenty of praise from others begging for leadership on the contentious issue.

Arizona may represent the front lines of state remedial action, but my experience as governor of Maryland represented a more traditional, if not less acrimonious, experience.

Indeed, the concentration of all stripes of notoriously progressive interest groups in the Maryland suburbs of Washington, D.C. made for plenty of high stakes conflict with yours truly. The outrage directed at me for opposing their multicultural agenda was matched by the outrageous nature of their alleged "rights": in no particular order, the right to have Maryland taxpayers fund a booklet that constituted a "how to" guide for evading capture by federal immigration officials, the right to receive in-state tuition breaks at Maryland's public colleges and universities,[29] and the right to secure a Maryland driver's license regardless of immigration status (a license that would not secure a seat on a commercial airliner). An added element to send the progressives and their media allies off the proverbial cliff was my wholesale rejection of "multiculturalism" (I referred to the concept as "bunk" and "crap") during a 2005 appearance on a Baltimore radio show.

It is a measure of how much ground a commonsense majority has lost that such issues have become a part of our political debate. But it should not be lost that these issues have fallen to the states because the federal government has failed to do its job. And the states pay for this failure every single day.

How much?

- The annual price tag to educate the children of illegal aliens is approximately $52 billion. The vast majority of these costs are piled up by local and state governments.[30]
- Illegal immigrants cost taxpayers approximately $113 billion a year. Of this sum, around $84 billion is paid by local and state governments.[31]
- An average of less than 5 percent of the social costs generated by illegal immigrants is recouped by local and state governments. (At the federal level, around one-third of public expenditures are recaptured.)[32]

In effect, state and local governments have been forced to cut back on legitimate state priorities (roads, corrections, K-12, community colleges) in order to subsidize illegal activity.

The fiscal downside of illegal immigration must play a pivotal role in the contentious debate over comprehensive immigration reform. It is a matter of fundamental fairness for taxpayers required to ante up more of their hard earned dollars to pay for the federal government's inaction and negligence.

The historic recession of 2007 could not have hit at a worse time. Talk about a double whammy: expenditures associated with illegal immigration skyrocketed just as a mortgage meltdown tanked tax collections at all levels of government. Is there any wonder why states have resorted to suing the federal government to do its job?

| CULTURE CHAPTER FOOTNOTES |

1. Douglas Murray, "Cameron's Multicultural Wake-Up Call," *The Wall Street Journal*, February 9, 2011.
2. Ibid.
3. Ibid.
4. Timothy Garton Ash, "What young British Muslims say can be shocking—some of it is also true," *The Guardian*, August 9, 2006.
5. Australian Prime Minister John Howard, "It's sense, not discrimination," *Daily Telegraph* (Sydney), September 2, 2006.
6. "Howard Australia's most Xenophobic Leader, Greens Say," ABC News Report, September 2, 2006.
7. Caitlin Gibson, "In Leesburg, holiday displays bring controversy and change," *The Washington Post*, December 16, 2011.
8. Peter Blair, "Church's 'Charlie Brown' Christmas play a casualty of culture wars," *The Washington Times*, December 6, 2012.
9. Texas Legislature, H.B. No. 308, http://www.capitol.state.tx.us/tlodocs/83R/billtext/html/HB00308I.htm
10. The historical literature is strong in this respect. The famous phrase "wall of separation" does not appear in the constitution. It was a phrase employed by Thomas Jefferson in a private letter to the

Danbury Baptist Association in 1802. Numerous scholars also point out that Jefferson attended services inside the House of Representatives presided over by any number of protestant ministers. So much for Jefferson's alleged impenetrable wall between church and state. See also Justice Rehnquist's dissent in *Wallace v. Jaffree*, wherein the future Chief Justice concludes that, "The 'wall of separation between church and State' is a metaphor based on bad history, a metaphor which has proved useless as a guide to judging. It should be frankly and explicitly abandoned."

11. Alex Pareene, "A New Declaration of Independence," *Salon*, October 30, 2011.
12. Jason Linkins, "Trying to Discern Occupy Wall Street's 'Demands? Think Jubilee," *Huffington Post*, October 5, 2011.
13. Sabrina Tavernise, "Married Couples No Longer a Majority, Census Finds," *The New York Times*, May 26, 2011.
14. National Womens' Law Center, "Poverty And Income Among Women And Families" (2000-2011); see also U.S. Census Bureau, Children's Living Arrangements and Characteristics: March 2002, pp. 20-547, Table C8. Washington, D.C.: GPO, 2003 (via The National Center For Fathering : The consequences of fatherlessness).
15. U.S. Department of Health and Human Services, National Center for Health Statistics, Survey on Child Health, Washington, DC; GPO, 1993 (via The National Center For Fathering : The consequences of fatherlessness).
16. Cynthia Harper and Sara S. McLanahan, cited in "Father Absence and Youth Incarceration," *Journal of Research on Adolescence* 14 (September 2004): pp. 369-397. (via The National Center For Fathering : The consequences of fatherlessness).
17. U.S. Department of Health and Human Services, Bureau of the Census, (via The National Center For Fathering : The consequences of fatherlessness).
18. United States Center for Disease Control (via The National Center For Fathering : The consequences of fatherlessness).
19. This point has been the topic of conversation during occasional conversations with major college football and basketball coaches. Without exception, these coach—mentors cite the lack of a father

or male influence as a major problem with so many of the recruited athletes.

20. "Did the Great Society ruin society?" Townhall.com, March 27,2013.

21. Walter E. Williams, "Our Real Problem is Cultural Decay, Not Guns," *Investors Buisness Daily,* February 12, 2013.

22. "Reid Calls Language Proposal Racist," *The Washington Times,* May 18, 2006.

23. Ibid.

24. "87% Say English Should be U.S. Official Language," Rasmussen Reports, May 11, 2010.

25. Ibid.

26. It seems clear that a combination of fencing and surveillance technology is the most logical and cost-effective strategy. Cost estimates to complete a 2,000 mile fence along the Mexican border range as high as 22.4 billion dollars. *New York Times,* October 19, 2011.

27. The case for such a plan is in: Al Cardenas (chairman of the American Conservative Union and Former chairman of the Florida Republican party), "Obama embraces default amnesty," *Washington Times,* January 26, 2012.

28. "Arizona Law Makers Say they Will Build A Fence," Foxnews.com/ Associated Press, November 24, 2011.

29. This issue was more recently subject to a statewide referendum in November 2012. Maryland voters approved the tuition break by a margin of 58% to 42%, thereby enhancing Maryland's reputation as a national leader in sanctuary status.

30. Jack Martin (Director of Special Projects) and Eric A. Ruark (Director of Research), "The fiscal burden of illegal immigration on United States taxpayers," Federation for American Immigration Reform, July 2010 (Revised Feb. 2011).

31. Ibid.

32. Ibid.

SEEKING ECONOMIC SECURITY

"In democracies, nothing is more great or more brilliant than commerce."

—ALEXIS DE TOCQUEVILLE

One of the obligatory chores of public life is to tour private businesses. Office holders are deluged with such visit requests, as businesses jockey to earn a prized visit from their councilman, congressman, or governor. These "field trips" are as much a part of politics as debates and 30-second attack ads. A typical venture into the real world of private enterprise would include an initial meeting with the corporate brass followed by the familiar walk-through across the factory, assembly line, or office floor. Periodic stops at specific work stations are scheduled in order to generate the ever-popular photo opportunity. Although impossible to count, I estimate close to a thousand such visits over twenty-four years of campaigns and public office. That's a lot of walking, chatting, and photos ops.

• • •

Field Trips

One striking aspect of these informational tours was the considerable pride in workmanship exhibited by the employees as I made stops along the tour. Despite the very brief time I had at each station, the designated employee was usually full of information about the task at hand. This enthusiasm extended to even menial assembly line tasks, often repetitive in nature. Yet, in my presence, these tasks were the object of intricate detail and great pride. At times, the tour leader would boast of the employee's long history with the firm. Mutual pride was evident in such workplaces where so many employees had enjoyed long tenures with a single employer. I left these visits with a renewed sense of optimism about our economy. Despite public attitudes to the contrary, we *still* manufactured goods and services in demand around the world. I saw it with my own eyes. Unfortunately, my periodic, positive experiences could not change public attitudes. It would always be the "big," well publicized numbers (unemployment rate, number of new jobs created, consumer confidence) that dictated public perception about the economy.

These field visits allowed the firm's leadership to educate me about their challenges, whether foreign or domestic. The educational sessions typically took place in a private meeting prior to the tour. This was also the time when the "ask" occurred, although probably too negative a term for the requests so often made to elected officials. In reality, most were of the run-of-the-mill variety:

Could you help arrange a meeting with an agency?

Would you sign on to a bill that will improve our bottom line?

Is it possible for you to meet with our trade association during our Washington "fly-in" week?

After the private chat, tours, and greetings, I would convey my thanks and encourage the leaders to keep in touch with regard to the issues we had discussed, including any required follow-up. And then I would move on to the next event on that day's schedule. Such is the drumbeat of retail politics in the modern age.

It was shortly after I entered Congress that the missing link in these never-ending field visits came to me; rarely did I have the opportunity to meet the back office folks, whether clerks, secretaries, janitors, or drivers. And on such occasions wherein I was able to meet these indispensable employees, the conversations were abbreviated. In effect, I had left too many businesses without having the opportunity to talk substance with those who may have liked and intended to support me, but who usually voted for the well-known (but anti-business) Democrat in the bluest of blue states. In effect, I was preaching to the choir in the board room, but walking right by the receptionist whose reflexive vote for down-ballot Democrats resulted in Maryland's well-earned reputation as one of America's most anti-business states.

The irony here is difficult to miss. So many of the businesses I visited were small technology firms engaged in the business of creating jobs for the next generation of American kids. The leadership more often than not understood the importance of a business-friendly environment, but the firm's employees were nevertheless consistently voting for the anti-business candidate from the dominant political party.

And herein lies one element of what's wrong with the American jobs-making machine: too many anti-business candidates are able to secure election to Congress. The vast majority have safe seats. Increasingly aggressive public sector union agendas dictate their votes. Nothing outside of a major scandal can place them in danger. Few ever feel political pressure to change their voting patterns. Many hail from coastal, solidly blue states that are insulated from the dangers of partisan realignment. Their reflexive votes along the progressive line are the source of daily frustration; their long careers on Capitol Hill (plus the unwillingness or inability of journalists to ask them tough questions regarding their anti-business voting patterns) present monumental obstacles to a pro-business Congressional majority and an American jobs revolution.

Small Business

The pitched battle between business and labor has played out in our politics from Day One, but it has been a more recent development that better defines the contours of today's small business challenges within Congress.

You see, an ascendant GOP circa 1994 adopted the small business community as representative of all that is right with America. A hotbed of friendly policy items followed: regulatory reform, paperwork reduction, capital gains and other business tax cuts, and healthcare overhaul were/are important planks in this policy initiative. The decision to further romanticize small business entrepreneurs was an easy one; some Members were small business owners themselves, while most of the new majority makers hailed from districts where the small business community was a potent, organized political force. It was the National Federation of Independent Business, the premier small business advocacy group, that set the small business agenda that became part of the "Contract With America." A new moniker ("Main Street, not Wall Street") set a rather populist tone for the new majority and its powerful constituency.

Democratic reaction was not so polite. This was a time when long-dominant liberal Democratic committee chairs had been forced to vacate their positions of power; a change few political pundits had thought likely prior to the fall of 1994. Seething resentment was a primary theme, as if Republicans had sneaked in during the night and stolen a favorite page from the Democratic leader's playbook. Worse, formerly shaken down small business interests were now liberated. Big dollars from these heretofore political captives began flowing toward the new pro (small) business majority.

This resentment has remained to this day, as NFIB and its allies rally the troops in opposition to the latest assault on economic freedom from the likes of Harry Reid and the Obama administration. And the NFIB congressional scorecard is always available to separate those who talk a good game from those who stand with small business owners during the most challenging of political times.

Educational Change

Another serious obstacle to private sector job creation is the educational divide, a gulf widely researched since the IT revolution of the early 1990s. The science with respect to educational "haves" and "have nots" speaks for itself:

- Higher educational attainment is directly linked to higher lifetime earnings;

- Annual earnings increase with successive degrees;
- Individuals with higher levels of education are more likely to be employed full-time.[1]

My hometown of Arbutus, Maryland provides appropriate context. The baby boom decade of the 1970s provides the appropriate timeline.

It was during this decade that one of the primary takeaways of the industrial revolution began to weaken: low tech skills would no longer lead to a middle class existence, and only a more educated workforce would enjoy the fruits of what a higher technology economy could supply. This was a most unsettling notion for working class America. Many of America's working class had grown up around large industrial plants that were the dominant employer in the area. In some places, these plants represented such an economic engine that entire communities developed around the local facility. For context, just think about the many suburban steel communities that popped up around the northeast and midwest during the 30s, 40s, and 50s. Jobs were plentiful, pay was good, and many carried minimal educational requirements. The work was labor intensive. Training regimes could be accomplished within weeks. Such knowledge could carry a good employee throughout his career and into a comfortable retirement.

As a suburban Baltimore kid, I knew many of the dads from my father's generation had followed this path: graduate from high school, secure a job at the local aluminum or steel mill, work for 35 years, and buy a retirement condo at the beach. The union-negotiated wage would be a ticket into the middle class, too. Not such a bad work cycle, *if* one survived the dangerous and dirty work environment.

That this worldview survived well into the computer age speaks to its powerful appeal—an appeal that survives in some rust belt states to this day. American industry dominated the world economy. Big-ticket American products were in demand. Detroit ruled the automobile industry. Organized labor was a dominant force within American politics. Cheaper, low-tech third world competition had yet to announce itself on the world stage. And a middle class lifestyle was available if one cared to wear a blue collar and put in eight grueling hours a day.

It was an era wherein management and labor grew comfortable with ever increasing sales, salaries, bonuses, and retirement packages. America enjoyed a trade surplus. A growing American middle class became the envy of the world. Few foresaw the crushing end to this prosperous era.

A Big Thud

The end did come, and it arrived with a serious thud. It was the 1980s, and suddenly corporate profits were down, legacy costs born of generous pension benefits for retired workers further squeezed corporate bottom lines, and cheaper foreign labor became a real threat. But it was the advent of the information age that caused the greatest turmoil. And in rust belt America, it was suddenly no longer acceptable to take that tenth grade education to the Bethlehem Steel or General Motors job fair.

As a Member of Congress representing a district with a major steel plant,[2] I *lived* the incremental decline of the industry, including periodic fights with those countries (China, Russia, Korea) whose unfair trade practices further accelerated the decline of the industry. In the end, the reality of a high-cost product, cheaper foreign labor, crushing legacy costs, and ineffective trade sanctions could not be stopped. Employment at Bethlehem Steel-Sparrows Point declined from a high of 36,000 in the 1960s to shut-down status today.[3] An inconvenient fact of (steel industry) life accompanied the dramatic decline in employment: labor productivity skyrocketed such that today far more steel can be produced with less than 10% of the workforce employed during the industrial era. Another contrast from my childhood: today's miniscule (by comparison) labor force is far more computer literate than thirty years ago. The bottom line moral is impossible to miss: education is no longer a perk in post-industrial America—it is a workplace necessity. Any message to the contrary merely harkens back to a romanticized past that will *never* return.

The D.C. Experience

The educational divide is further exacerbated by the firm resistance of the educational establishment (read: teachers' unions) to support extraordinary remedies in under-performing school systems. And there is no better recent example than the continuing broadsides from the Obama administration aimed at the District of Columbia Scholarship Program.

The popular program (which falls under Congressional jurisdiction) allows impoverished children in the notoriously under-performing D.C. public school system to attend area private schools with vouchers of up to $12,000. Its contentious history reflects full-scale support from Congressional Republicans and the George W. Bush administration. Unfortunately, but not surprisingly, it took but a few short months for a new Obama administration to pull the plug on new applicants in 2009. The scheduled termination of the program was just another sop to an anti-school—choice teachers union from an NEA-friendly President.

Today's politics are marked by short-term, turbulent election cycles, however. And so it was that the 2010 mid-term elections brought a new House GOP majority to Capitol Hill. Shortly thereafter, pro-voucher Speaker Boehner was quick to include $20 million (over five years) in voucher aid as an integral part of his 2011 spending deal with a still resistant administration. [4]

Talk about the difference one election can make: one new House majority, one new House Speaker, hundreds of poor, mostly African-American schoolchildren (again) provided the opportunity to choose quality over monopoly, and thousands of relieved, often tearful parents filled with gratitude.

This emotionalism is not surprising. The program remains quite popular. Public opinion polls reflect clear majority support within the District. And there is a reason for such public support. Objective analysis from a variety of well-respected investigators (including the Obama administration's Education Department research arm) reflects what common sense would lead one to suspect: voucher recipients score better on standardized reading tests and enjoy substantially higher graduation rates as compared to their peers in the D.C. public schools.

Simply put, the program works.

Nevertheless, the Obama administration came up with an election year attempt to gin up its left flank by zeroing out voucher funding in its fiscal 2013 budget. The targeted beneficiaries: teachers unions and their anti-voucher allies in Congress. One especially troubling provision prohibited students who were unsuccessful in the program's lottery from reapplying the next year. For anyone who has seen the raw emotional responses of parents to the news of their child's selection into (or rejection from) the program, this is a particularly nasty step in the wrong direction.

There are those public school advocates who oppose any form of public school choice. They view any option outside of the traditional public school setting as detrimental and in direct contradiction to the role of public education. Their answer to the many ills besetting so many of our underperforming school systems never changes: "give 'em more money." And so we have, at every level of government.

But times are changing. Governments are stretched for cash. Taxpayers are demanding ever more accountability. The time for more money has come and gone. Dysfunctional school systems require fundamental change. Time has shown that good money after bad is *not* the answer.

Today, advocates of school choice come in many varieties: black and white, urban and rural, liberal and conservative, Democrat and Republican. They are increasingly willing to take a chance—to choose "all of the above" —when it comes to the education of our most challenging students.

In the District of Columbia (and other under-performing school systems), one of the "above" options is to give (some) poor kids a shot at a private school education. It is an opportunity to punch a ticket at a place that will nurture their intellectual skills. Of course, not everyone who applies is chosen; this one program is not the *only* answer to our considerable educational challenges. But it is a part of the answer. Many rightly see the voucher program as their best opportunity to escape the pull of multigenerational poverty. Let's hope the leader who so convincingly talks about compassion will (eventually) find some for a group of vulnerable kids living in his backyard.

The Regulatory Mindset

One of today's most discouraging obstacles to job creation is the crushing regulatory assault on small business job creators by government at all levels. Talk to a small business owner and you will receive an earful about paperwork and attitude; and it's the latter that contributes to problems with the former. The attitude referenced herein refers to the onerous approach often undertaken by government regulators. That such attitudes can fester during severe economic downturns speaks to the overarching arrogance of the regulatory state.

In the real world, regulatory approaches fall into two general categories: (1.) partner; or (2.) sheriff. A partnership does not presuppose business is always right and government always wrong. Far from it. There *are* unscrupulous business owners who have little regard for the law. Some seek profit to the exclusion of everything else. Others turn a blind eye toward the poisoning of our fragile ecosystems. They are a distinct minority, but they do exist. Regulators, law enforcement, and prosecutors are in business to deal with the likes of them.

The vast majority of small business people are simply attempting to make ends meet. Their goals are simple: pay the bills, make a buck, and (hopefully) grow their business. Some have borrowed money or taken a second mortgage in order to follow their dream. They *deserve* a willing partner.

Ideally, a partner-regulator will advise and guide them through the regulatory morass that awaits all entrepreneurs. This bureaucrat abhors regulatory "gotcha." Instead, he is all about keeping his taxpayer-clients out of trouble. Such is the job description the freight-paying public deserves. Unfortunately, it is not the business model advocated by the modern left. Today's progressives believe government agencies must adopt the sheriff mode, constantly on the prowl for employer-lawbreakers who must be punished. This mentality values notches on its regulatory holster; every fine, sanction, or indictment justifies its existence, and feeds its insatiable search for employer-miscreants.

The Obama administration is a prime example of this value system in action. Few of its primary policy makers can point to distinguished private sector careers; its Cabinet rates historically low in private sector experience.[5] Its primary workplace regulators are viscerally anti-employer, with OSHA and the National Labor Relations Board the lead sheriffs in ramping up workplace enforcement efforts while implementing organized labor's policy agenda through a blizzard of new regulations.

An EPA Sheriff

There is no better example of this mindset than the controversy surrounding the April 20, 2012 resignation of Assistant EPA Administrator Al Armendariz. Mr. Armendariz had the unfortunate experience of having a heretofore undisclosed video of a particularly bellicose 2010 speech on EPA enforcement practices surface in the midst of a tense presidential campaign.

In comments concerning non-compliant oil and gas company targets, Armendariz arrogantly analogized EPA supervision of the alleged miscreant firms to "when the Romans conquered the villages in the Mediterranean. They'd go into little villages in Turkish towns and they'd find the first five guys they saw and crucify them."[6] This overtly belligerent view from a high ranking environmental regulator caught the immediate attention of Congressional Republicans and further confirmed the worst fears of the business community about the Obama administration's "real" agenda.

A subsequent apology for his "poor choice of words" failed to placate his critics, however. GOP leaders (led by Senator James Inhofe) rejected the expression of regret. No surprise here. "Smoking gun" admissions from senior officials are never lightly dismissed, particularly in Washington, D.C. The chapter was closed when Armendariz submitted his letter of resignation a few days later.

Labor Policy

The issues that dictate the tenor of job creation initiatives and labor—management relations lie primarily within the executive branch. And this is clearly one area wherein the Obama administration delivered on its promise of "hope and change." Only in this case, the change could not have been more damaging to job creation, as America stumbles along at an unemployment rate in excess of 7% and with more than six million workers qualifying as long term unemployed. As for hope, it has given way to the realities of Big Labor's policy initiatives. Further, businesses feel the hostility from labor-friendly regulators; the nation's job creators will continue to proceed with great caution during the Obama era.

Too many American businesses are not in hiring mode despite reports of healthy balance sheets, plenty of cash reserves, and optimistic forecasts. And one major reason is the Obama administration's hard left tilt toward the most progressive elements of organized labor since "Day One" of its tenure.

ITEM: In February 2009 the President signed an Executive Order mandating the use of "Project Labor Agreements" (PLAs) on public construction projects around the country. The order overturned a Bush administration order which had banned the use of PLAs. Such agreements mandate the use of union-only labor (in exchange for labor "peace" and timely completion) and increase the costs associated with big ticket construction projects.

ITEM: In April 2011 the National Labor Relations Board started a regulatory firestorm by filing a controversial complaint to block the Boeing Corporation from completing a new aircraft assembly line in South Carolina, a right-to-work state. The NLRB was unhappy the new line would not be completed in union-friendly Washington State. Only after considerable concessions were made to Boeing's machinists' union did the federal agency agree to drop the complaint. The agency's "union line" warning to corporate America could not have been clearer.

ITEM: In May 2011 the Chicago director of the NLRB ruled that St. Xavier University, a Catholic college located in Chicago, was not sufficiently religious to be exempt from federal jurisdiction. The decision followed a similar ruling against another jurist institution, Manhattan College.

ITEM: In June 2011 the Obama Labor Department issued a proposal that would require employers to publish additional information about the independent labor consultants employed to oppose union organizing activities. One problem: the proposed rule would *not* limit the union's right to hire whatever attorney or consultant they wished to engage. The predictable result: consultants hired by employers will find far fewer opportunities for work—and employers will find themselves with one less tool in their workplace arsenal. Alas, some of the anti-business biases of the left are the result of unintended consequences; some are quite intended.

ITEM: Also in June 2011 the NLRB proposed regulations that would shorten the time between a formal call for a union vote and an organizing election. The proposed change would provide less time for employers to prepare for an election, presumptively tilting the playing field in favor of union organizers.

ITEM: So-called "card check" legislation was a focal point of organized labor's legislative wish list at the beginning of the Obama administration. Support for the bill (which would have ended secret ballots in union organizing elections) gave added impetus to labor's hyper-aggressive push to elect Obama during the 2008 campaign. Fortunately, even a Democratic Congress refused to go along with the bill's ill-advised attempt to disenfranchise American workers in the workplace. Continued GOP control of at least one House of Congress assures this bad policy will not become law anytime soon, despite the best efforts of the President and the Democratic leadership.

Missing Opportunities

The Obama administration's presumptive tilt toward a regulatory mindset also carried the day in two instances wherein the president (unfortunately) resisted entreaties from organized labor: the proposed 7 billion dollar Keystone pipeline project and exploration of the Arctic National Wildlife Refuge (ANWR).

The proposed cross-border pipeline would run from the oil sands of Alberta, Canada to the Texas gulf coast. Upon completion, the pipeline would carry 800,000 barrels of oil per day.[7] The economic benefits include thousands of new construction and manufacturing jobs.[8] The new pipeline would provide the U.S. with a safe and secure source of energy. It would bolster bilateral relations with our friendly northern neighbor. It would help wean us off of our over-dependence on unstable, autocratic regimes in the Middle East. Politically, it binds business and labor interests together in common cause; a regular occurrence whenever extreme environmental policy seeks to kill what would be newly-generated union jobs. The proposed pipeline would appear to be an easy sell for a country addicted to purchasing its energy from unfriendly and unreliable regimes. But what is a no-brainer for the average American has been a non-starter for the Obama administration. Years of study and positive State Department reviews still have the President and his Environmental Protection Agency in pipeline delay mode.[9] And a new post-election litmus test ("significant" impact on global warming) has proponents of the project pessimistic about ultimate approval.

The issue of exploration within the Coastal Plain of the Arctic National Wildlife Refuge is equally familiar to those who follow energy policy. The Carter administration purchased this land in part due to its high oil reserves. As a Member of Congress assigned to the Commerce Committee, I took the opportunity to visit the North Slope and learn firsthand about an issue that has bounced around Congress since the 1980 Alaska National Interest Lands Conservation Act.

The trip was quite instructive. The proposed drilling footprint is small—less than 3% of ANWR's total acreage. Newly developed, state-of-the-art drilling technology will make the footprint substantially smaller. The area was set aside specifically for oil and natural gas exploration. It was *never* a designated wilderness area. Indeed, the area is primarily dreary, barren wasteland. I've seen it with my own eyes. Legislation that would allow ANWR drilling has passed the House of Representatives twelve times! Yet, the area remains untouched to this day. And a second-term Obama administration means there is no relief in sight.

The Long View

Sometimes it is worth our time to step back and take the long view about seemingly intractable issues impacting our country.

My long view begins with the gas line days of 1973-74, when a recently minted owner of a 1966 Ford Falcon began the long daily commute between his home in the western suburbs of

Baltimore to and from Gilman School in northwest Baltimore. Domestically, huge price hikes at the pump and draconian gas rationing (remember the "even-odd" license plate system?) nearly destroyed new automobile sales, a crushing burden for a father employed as a commission-only car salesman. Fortunately, the Ehrlichs survived; we also took notice as leaders from both major parties promised "never again" would an OPEC cartel impose its will on a defenseless America; "never again" would hostile regimes be in a position to inflict such damage on the world's most vibrant economy; "never again" would our leadership fail in its duty to develop safe and secure sources of energy for the American people.

Subsequent years have brought great change to the oil producing nations of the Middle East: periodic civil wars, a virulent strain of radical Islam, an emergent Muslim Brotherhood, the Arab Spring (initial outcome disquieting, but final results still to be determined), and ever increasing tensions with Israel are just a few of the geo-political chapters of its recent past.

What has not changed is America's continued reliance on sources of oil from increasingly unstable (and sometimes unfriendly) nations. This fact of energy policy-life represents a monumental failure of political will. It also invites further instability in an unsettled region. Today, the world watches nervously as Iran supports Assad in Syria and escalates its anti-Israel rhetoric and saber-rattling ways in the Gulf of Hormuz.

A series of major domestic policy failures are to blame. And an inconvenient truth is at the center of the controversy: the ability of our economy to grow new jobs is dependent on available and inexpensive sources of energy. For the foreseeable future, those sources (primarily natural gas and oil) are fossil fuel driven. Technological progress with respect to shale gas exploration further strengthens the notion. But the flipside is not so promising: the "green jobs revolution" so ardently promoted by progressives will not arrive anytime soon; wind, solar, and biodiesel must be promoted and explored, but will not produce the source supply required to sustain a growing economy over the next 10-15 years. That some on the progressive left will take issue with this last statement is a certainty. This group tends to embellish when it comes to green job production and the U.S. economy, notwithstanding the Obama Department of Energy's embarrassing experiences with the likes of Solyndra and Abound Solar Inc. The green lobby's optimistic projections certainly make for pithy sound bites on the campaign trail. But recent testimony from the Bureau of Labor Statistics buttresses the view that the advent of a serious green jobs revolution is still a way off.

A Tall (Green) Tale

The background was a June 8, 2012 House oversight hearing led by Chairman Darryl Issa of California. The topic was a hot button issue sure to inflame partisan passions: how the federal government goes about the business of counting green jobs. The main witnesses were Bureau of Labor Statistics Acting Commissioner Josh Galvin and Assistant Secretary for Employment and Training Jane Oates. Mr. Galvin's unhappiness with being called in front of the Committee was barely contained, but it was a startling series of questions and answers that produced the most revealing testimony of the day.

> REP. DARRELL ISSA: Well, let me—let me run you through some questions here because you're here because we're having a green jobs counting discussion. Does someone who assembles turbines—is that a green job?

MS. JANE OATES: Wind turbines?

REP. ISSA: Yeah. Wind turbines.

MS. OATES: I think we would call any kind of sustainable manufacturing –

REP. ISSA: OK.

MS. OATES:—fitting the definition that was –

REP. ISSA: Does someone who sweeps—does someone who sweeps the floor in a facility that makes solar panels, is that a green job?

MS. OATES: Solar? I'll give that to –

REP. ISSA: To Galvin?

MS. OATES:—if you don't mind.

MR. JOHN GALVIN: We define—we have a two-part definition –

REP. ISSA: We already had the briefing on that. So just answer the question. If you're sweeping the floor in a solar panel production facility, is that a green job?

MR. GALVIN: If you ask me for the number of health care jobs in the United States, I'll give you the employment from the health care industry.

REP. ISSA: Look, Mr. Galvin –

MR. GALVIN:—nurses and doctors –

REP. ISSA: You did not want to come here as a witness. You are not a delighted witness. So let's go through this. I asked you a question. You know the answer. Would you please answer it? If you sweep the floor in a solar panel facility, is that a green job?

MR. GALVIN: Yes.

REP. ISSA: Thank you. If you drive a hybrid bus—public transportation—is that a green job?

MR. GALVIN: According to our definition, yes.

REP. ISSA: Thank you. What if you're a college professor teaching classes about environmental studies?

MR. GALVIN: Yes.

REP. ISSA: What about just any school bus driver?

MR. GALVIN: Yes.

REP. ISSA: What about the guy who puts gas in the school bus?

MR. GALVIN: Yes.

REP. ISSA: How about employees at a bicycle shop?

MR. GALVIN: I guess I'm not sure about that.

REP. ISSA: The answer is yes, according to your definition. And you've got a lot of them. What about a clerk at the bicycle repair shop?

MR. GALVIN: Yes.

REP. ISSA: What about someone who works in an antique dealer?

MR. GALVIN: I'm not sure about that either.

REP. ISSA: The answer is yes. Those are—those are recycled goods. They're antiques; they're used. What about someone who works at the Salvation Army in their clothing recycling and furniture?

MR. GALVIN: Right. Because they're selling recycled goods.

REP. ISSA: OK. What about somebody who opened a store to sell rare manuscripts?

MR. GALVIN: What industry is that?

REP. ISSA: People sell rare books and manuscripts—but they're rare because they're old so they're used.

MR. GALVIN: OK.

REP. ISSA: What about workers at a consignment shop?

MR. GALVIN: That's a green job.

REP. ISSA: Does the teenage kid who works full time at a used record shop count?

MR. GALVIN: Yes.

REP. ISSA: How about somebody who manufactures railroads rolling stock—basically, train cars?

MR. GALVIN: I don't think we classified the manufacture of rail cars as –

REP. ISSA: 48.8 percent of jobs in manufacturing, rail cars counted, according to your statistics. About half of the jobs that are being used to build trains. OK. How about—just one more here. What about people who work in a trash disposal yard? Do garbage men have green jobs?

MR. GALVIN: Yes.

REP. ISSA: OK. I apologize. The real last last is, how about an oil lobbyist? Wouldn't an oil lobbyist count as having a green job if they are engaged in advocacy related to environmental issues?

MR. GALVIN: Yes.[10]

Such illuminating testimony from a hostile witness is relatively rare on Capitol Hill. But the abject silliness of the job categorizations was a stark reminder about how far afield some bureaucrats, and politicians, will go to promote an agenda.

A brief reminder for the green motivated crowd— all of us look forward to the day America becomes energy self-reliant. Green innovation will surely assist in reaching that goal. But fudging commonsense definitions in order to support a political objective doesn't cut it. It's dishonest, it leads to bad policy decisions, and it's just embarrassing.

Green Reality

Some on the right contend the Obama appointees currently in charge of environmental policy are quietly pleased (even if the President himself has not openly admitted such) to see gas hovering in the neighborhood of $4 per gallon. Such anti-"growthers" abhor consumption. They ask why America should be so different from Europe, where the price of gasoline in Germany tops $8 per gallon. Some are happy to advocate for a less consumption-driven standard of living, too. A few, such as former Obama administration Green Czar Van Jones, have been quite open in their dislike for cheaper oil. Few would deny that the President and Mr. Jones are of identical mindsets when it comes to the issue of low gas prices.

Today, everyone talks about the need for safe and secure sources of oil and natural gas. But so many politicians lack the ability to move forward; to make a decision. Their platitudes only proliferate during campaign season. The old political adage applies: "politicians *talk the talk*, leaders *walk the walk.*" And without more walking, our addiction to unstable and (often) unfriendly sources of energy bodes ill for long-term national energy security.

Ideological Differences

There remain, however, significant differences between the parties. And it does not take a political science major to figure it all out. One of the most important concerns the role of government in the workplace. A visceral distrust of the marketplace and a frequent ignorance of its exigencies lead most Democrats to the "sheriff mode" and a harsh regulatory approach to workplace issues. Conversely, a market-friendly GOP endorses the partnership model of accommodation when possible, and sanctions when required. Hopefully, a commonsense consensus will emerge wherein reasonable regulation will no longer act to the detriment of economic growth.

At the end of the day, it comes down to trust, and whether one places more trust in government or the private sector. All parties need to keep in mind that workplace safety is not mutually exclusive of workplace efficiency, however. We can (and must) have both. A bit more cooperation from both sides of the aisle would help, but the irresponsibility award for this era goes to progressive Democrats for their overly zealous approach to marketplace regulation. Their attitude costs us jobs. Their policies are counter-productive. Their egalitarian values make our economic future less secure.

The Bottom Line:
Diminishing Entrepreneurship

That progressive interest groups are inflicting great damage on the (previously) romantic notion of the self-made entrepreneur is an irrefutable takeaway from this tome. America no longer celebrates small business success stories like we used to.

Economists and pundits alike have taken notice. Recent economic data suggests that entrepreneurial risk taking is on the decline, as are start-up ventures and the number of existing businesses wishing to expand their operations."[11]

These trend lines can be explained away in any number of ways. Fewer hours, less risk, and more guaranteed benefits are typically associated with larger (as opposed to smaller) businesses. But the negative impact of the cultural messaging from today's progressives cannot be ignored. The chants are familiar: capitalism is mean, private equity types are meaner, and wouldn't it be so much better if we could achieve a more "just" society. The President of the United States just told me so, on television, in thousands of paid ads during the 2012 campaign. And . . . where do I get my free (Obama) phone?

Despite recent progress, progressivism will not change the laws of economics. One such law concerns the outsized number of jobs generated when small businesses grow into large businesses. (Think Apple, Under Armour, Intel). Which begs a question: can a more progressive America produce enough entrepreneurial success stories to sustain its standard of living? The trend lines are presently negative. The Obama regulatory state is ascendant. And it will require a Reagan-esque revolution to restore our momentum. But it *can* be done.

| ECONOMIC AND ENERGY CHAPTER FOOTNOTES |

1. College Board Advocacy & Policy Center, Trends in Higher Education, trends.collegeboard.org/meny/highlights-1.
2. In 1959, Bethlehem Steel-Sparrows Point claimed title to the largest steelworks in the world. See: Deborah Rudacille, "In the Shadow of Steel," *Urbanite Baltimore Magazine,* April 1, 2010.
3. Hanah Cho, "Sparrows Point is Shutting Down," *The Baltimore Sun,* May 25, 2012.
4. Resistant is perhaps too benign a term. A teachers' union-friendly Obama then zeroed-out funding for the program in his subsequent budget. Alas, discretionary Department of Education dollars represent a short term compromise.
5. Michael Cembalest, "Obama's Business Blind Spot," *Forbes,* November 24, 2009. For a critical view of Cembalest's work, see Politifact.com, September 27, 2012.
6. Les Jansen and Todd Sperry, "EPA Official Resigns Over Crucify Remark," CNN.com, April 30, 2012.
7. Nicolas Loris, "Obama's 'Forced' Keystone Decision Rejects Jobs, Energy, and Logic," *The Heritage Foundation,* January 18, 2012.
8. Ibid.
9. Ibid.
10. Nicholas Ballasy, "Labor Dept. counts oil lobbyists, garbage men, bus drivers as 'green jobs'," *The Daily Caller,* June 8, 2012. http://dailycaller.com/2012/06/08/labor-dept-counts-oil-lobbyists-garbage-men-bus-drivers-as-green-jobs-video/#ixzz2DMMp5F4F
11. Ben Casselman, "Risk-Averse Culture Infects U.S. Workers, Entrepreneurs, *The Wall Street Journal,* June 2, 2013.

NATIONAL SECURITY *and* OUR NATIONAL IDENTITY

"The ultimate determinant in the struggle now going on for the world will not be bombs and rockets but a test of wills and ideas—a trial of spiritual resolve; the values we hold, the beliefs we cherish and the ideas to which we are dedicated."

—RONALD REAGAN

E very American recalls where he or she was on September 11, 2001, when first told terrorists had crashed hijacked commercial airliners into high profile targets in the U.S . It was immediately clear to those with some political sophistication that America was at war. What we could not understand at that point was the nature of the new threat. That was quickly revealed, however, and America's role in the world changed in dramatic fashion. But the patriotic enthusiasm that fueled our post 9/11 military invasions sure seems like a long time ago. So long ago, the Obama administration, it seems, has all but forgotten what fueled our response in the wake of the attacks on our country. All of which presents a big problem: the loosely affiliated confederation of bad guys continues to recruit and they still want to kill us. And the fact that they tend to think in terms of *centuries* rather than *years* makes our task all the more difficult.

Our complacency fuels their terror. Our laziness and comfort breeds attacks. The horror of April 15, 2013 just feet from the finish line of the Boston Marathon, on Patriots Day, is proof that ramping up our diligence cannot happen only after we are hit. We can never take our eye off of the ball. Small but deadly attacks like this one are the new threat; domestic assaults in the Western world are now a near constant.

September 11, 2001

One of my more interesting Congressional duties was to serve as a *deputy whip* for our Republican House majority under Speaker Dennis Hastert. The title was somewhat sexier than the job itself: it's simply not a lot of fun trying to lobby recalcitrant Members to vote leadership's way on upcoming legislation. Some were contrary just to be contrary; some had a "fear of commitment," trying to avoid taking positions that would open them to any criticism at all; and some were uncooperative because they wished to maintain their "free agent" status, that is, until they were challenged in primaries and suddenly needed to be a part of the team.

Nevertheless, I enjoyed the weekly meetings with my fellow deputy whips. It gave me an opportunity to catch up with my friends, learn about how politics was practiced in congressional districts around the country, and (at times) vent about the latest slanders inflicted on the long-suffering Republicans of Maryland. Every so often our meetings would include "sit downs" with the President's Congressional liaisons and senior staff.

Our House Whip delegation arrived at the White House for our fall agenda meeting with the President's staff around 8am that fateful morning. The meeting proceeded in the normal course for the next 75 minutes until we were informed that a second jet (we had not been notified about the first) had hit the World Trade

Center. We were told to return immediately to Capitol Hill. The chaotic scene at the White House that day is forever etched in my memory: staffers running to and from their cars and bewildered police trying to piece together what was unfolding at the nearby Pentagon.

The scene on Capitol Hill was more of the same, as the smoke from the Pentagon attack could be seen from my third floor window in the Cannon House Office Building. Shortly thereafter, the Capitol Hill Police stopped by to order us out of the building. Their instructions: find the quickest way out of town (the Congressional leadership had already helicoptered out of town to that soon-to-be-infamous "undisclosed location"). Accordingly, we closed the office and soon joined a monumental traffic jam along North Capitol Street headed to the Maryland suburbs. It was another four hours before I completed the 35-mile drive home to nearby Timonium, Maryland where I found an anxious wife (and two-year-old son) glued to our basement television.

Generational Influences

As a post-Vietnam kid growing up in peacetime (my high school graduation occurred two years after US withdrawal and the end of the draft), my generation was not so traumatized by the tenor and tone of the 1960s. Indeed, young men a mere four years older than I had come of age during a sexual revolution, emerging drug culture, civil rights protests, the draft, and Kent State. It was a time when major cities burned and many college campuses were transformed into hotbeds of anti-war sentiment. Cultural trauma defined the decade; few grew up during a more tumultuous time in US history. Hollywood will make movies about "the 60s" for decades to come.

My generation? Well, many of my peers seemed more preoccupied with disco, marijuana, and graduate school. It was the 70s and America was catching its breath after a decade of social and cultural upheaval. There was one indisputable fact of our formative years, however: military adventurism of the Vietnam variety would be on the wane. My generation would witness two significant military draw-downs: both the post-Vietnam and post-Cold War eras may have been characterized by continuing social and economic change, but not so much by repercussions of a shooting war.

The dawn of a new decade brought another revolution, but this time a conservative one. The 1980s, born with a new patriotism heralded in by a "miracle on ice" at the Lake Placid Olympics and Ronald Reagan's "morning in America" presidency, proved that the United States was not going to remain mired in foreign policy weakness pursuant to a Vietnam hangover or the aberrant Jimmy Carter presidency. (Indeed, those four years—my college years—born of war fatigue and suspicion towards the aborted Nixon presidency, led the way for many to a rebirth of "love of country," the harbinger of the "Reagan era.")

The new Republican president immediately set about the business of restoring American pride. America was again in business with a domestic program of growth orientated tax cuts and entrepreneurism and a foreign policy laser focused on a mischievous evil empire. And the best part, at least for us young activists, was that a hostile media just could not get the American public to dislike the movement conservative firmly ensconced in the White House.

That the Reagan presidency extended an additional four years under the more moderate George Herbert Walker Bush is by-and-large accurate, but even a Cold War victory over the Soviet Union and high tech take down of Saddam Hussein's war machine in the Persian Gulf could not extend it another four years. The era came to an abrupt end with the election of self-proclaimed southern "moderate" Bill Clinton.

The ambitious Clinton had indeed governed Arkansas as one might expect of a southern Democrat. In Washington, he even claimed, but never convincingly, that "the era of big government was over."[1] But what was not so moderate during the early Clinton years was the proposed federal takeover of American healthcare led by First Lady Hillary Clinton. This signature initiative of the Clinton administration was controversial from *Day One*. The secret deliberations and controversial policy determinations within *Hillarycare* energized the conservative heartland, as many political novices recognized an opportunity to derail the *Hillarycare Express* in the mid-term elections. And so it was that so many first time candidates won election to Congress in 1994, as Republicans took control of the House of Representatives for the first time in 40 years.

1994

The election of 1994 marked a turning point in recent political history. Newt Gingrich was suddenly the most popular Republican in the country. The GOP's *Contract With America* dominated the domestic agenda. A huge freshman class (yours truly included) arrived in Washington with a revolutionary zeal and a willingness to break eggs. Some Members were first-time candidates with no political experience. There were more doctors and business people than lawyers. The collective goal was to change Washington, *not* become a part of its culture. And many of us were Reagan-inspired 30-somethings committed to shoring up our national defense precisely because we had come of age during this time of relative peace and introspection. The anti-military presumptions of a slightly older generation were now replaced by an enthusiastic buy-in on behalf of a military build-up. Even those (like me) who had not served possessed this decidedly pro-military bent; our formative years were marked by a historic Cold War victory achieved without firing a shot.

This militaristic resolve was strengthened by the terror attacks of September 11, 2001. Our post-attack, closed-door briefings with Secretaries Donald Rumsfeld and Colin Powell reinforced the view that we were at war with a diabolical enemy engaged in a prolonged terror war against the West. Previous attacks on American and western interests around the world provided context for our views. The incidents were always noted and the worst of them (Marine barracks in Beirut; US embassies in Africa; USS Cole) would from time-to-time provoke a limited military response. But the big picture was always missing. Few attempted to piece it all together. Fewer still observed what was there for all to see: the United States (and the civilized world) was at war with various iterations of radical Islam.

As a post-9/11 America emerged, the picture was less than ideal. Our intelligence had failed. Our borders were leaky. And now our people were nervous. It was fear of the unknown that caused so many sleepless nights: if a low-tech attack by a small group of terrorists could inflict such damage, what high tech atrocities would they turn to next? And would fear of another terrorist attack on American soil come to rule our culture for years to come?

War Lessons

While these and many more perplexing security-related questions were being asked at home, a briefly united America entered into shooting wars in Iraq and Afghanistan. Saddam Hussein's weapons of mass destruction in Iraq and the presence of terrorist training camps in Afghanistan were the respective US targets. But a series of strategic miscalculations in both campaigns provided cause to recalibrate our earlier observations regarding US military capacities in the new millennium.

In Iraq, there was the predictable sectarian violence that broke out in the aftermath of our lightning quick "victory." The administrative and military misjudgments that followed contributed to the deaths of more than 4,000 American troops after President Bush's now infamous "Mission Accomplished" speech on the deck of the USS Abraham Lincoln on May 1, 2003. The ultimate failure to locate weapons of mass destruction magnified our political retrospective about the need to invade in the first place. Of course, retrospective here is but another name for 20/20 hindsight. Nevertheless, there are many of us who might have been less acquiescent about our Iraqi war vote if the intelligence regarding Saddam's WMD had been accurate.[2]

Another reason for our aggressive view was America's previous experience with the Iraqi military. The first Gulf War was an unqualified success for America and its allied coalition. The relative ease with which Saddam Hussein's invading army was expelled from Kuwait gave rise to a hyper-confident, technology superior worldview. Explosive proof of this technological advantage was beamed to America's living rooms every evening. Here, America could watch in awe as General Norman Schwarzkopf conducted daily press conferences wherein the latest, greatest US weapons were put on very public display. It was less boots on the ground than sorties in the air. And those amazingly accurate strikes against what at the time was the fifth largest army in the world created a strong impression that America's unsurpassed military might would ensure a low casualty, rapid victory war environment for the foreseeable future.

Only those more intimately familiar with the complexities of modern warfare gave thought to the significant differences between open desert warfare and the close quarters, guerilla combat that defined so many Iraqi campaign battles. Further, this time, Saddam the brutal dictator was literally fighting for his life, a fight he lost in December 2006.

Conversely, Afghanistan presented a less daunting retrospective. After all, this was the place where al-Qaeda fighters trained for the 9/11 attacks. The goal of keeping the bad guys pinned down there rather than here presented a far more compelling rationale for sustained engagement in that godforsaken country. In this respect, even anti-war candidate Obama had taken great pains to distinguish between the Bush administration's "war of choice" in Iraq and "war of necessity" in Afghanistan.

Other problematic factors have contributed to our post 9-11 learning curve: our ability to create and sustain a reasonably effective government in a historically tribal country such as Afghanistan; the degree of popular support for US aid as manifested by the indigenous population; the American populace's unhappiness with casualties sustained in seemingly endless wars; and the ability of our 24/7 news cycle to shape often negative political opinions about war.

This last point bears additional analysis as Americans seek to "win" a war far different from other major conflicts in our country's history. A war without opposing uniforms and organized armies, a war fought as much by domestic police agencies as trained soldiers. The military refers to such engagements as "asymmetrical," as in unique rules for a unique war fought in unique ways. For the average person in the real world, it translates into a difficult-to-grasp concept: periodic drone kills of militants in the tribal regions of Afghanistan, Pakistan, and Sudan simply do not translate into sustained positive media reports in the way major battlefield victories used to do. The President's insistence on a date certain for complete US withdrawal further complicates the equation. This non-negotiable condition makes it more difficult to define "victory" or even "success" in such circumstances.

The Role of Social Media

Casualty-intensive setbacks on the battlefield or in allegedly government controlled towns and cities now receive real-time coverage in this Twitter and Facebook world. Of course, social media may have played a constructive role in the development of the Arab Spring, but it just as easily conveys the myriad complexities and lack of progress attendant to changing the hearts and minds of a populace not heretofore exposed to democratic traditions and institutions, let alone a functioning central government. Moreover, social media can have a misleading evidentiary effect. We may never know how representative were the democratic inferences from the social media in play during the Arab Spring. Certainly, Mohamed Morsi's attempt to jam through an Islamist constitution enraged secular Egyptians, ultimately to the demise of his presidency. The bottom line: an ascendant Brotherhood failed to warm the hearts (or hopes) of western democrats.

Similarly, the speed of cyberspace can make truly horrific events immediately understandable—and even more impactful. Witness the incalculable damage done to the allied nation-building campaign in Iraq in the aftermath of Abu Ghraib, where American mistreatment of captured enemy combatants was readily telecast to an already indignant Muslim world. For contrast, ponder how much quicker our "pacification" campaign in Vietnam would have been tarnished once rumors of the My Lai massacre hit cyberspace.

Imagine the impact on some of the more draconian decisions made in past wars by our most revered war leaders: Would the British decision to bomb German civilian targets stand up to our current media frenzy? Would Churchill be vilified as a war criminal instead? Would media coverage of 6,000 killed, wounded and missing at Normandy[3] withstand today's hypercritical punditry? How many times would a horrified Congress have required Eisenhower to explain himself? Similarly, could Lincoln have survived the punditry after public consumption of the carnage at Gettysburg?

The bottom line: today's real time communications make the reporting of wartime atrocities more immediately damaging to the political leadership. In effect, war in all its horror has a new public relations problem, which may, come to think of it, be the single best thing I can observe about social media.

Pay Any Price?

Does the United States (and the West) possess the internal fortitude to defeat contemporary enemies such as al-Qaeda and its progeny?

This question crosses my mind whenever I'm exposed to the "peace groups" that occasionally pop up on television news or appear at local Fourth of July parades. Their signs and banners reflect emotional demands for peace on behalf of a war-weary country fighting a loosely aligned confederation of Islamic extremists spread throughout the world. My immediate thought: how these well-meaning folks process reports such as al-Qaeda's recent poster campaign promising to make a return mass casualty engagement in New York City. Do they sincerely wish to placate or ignore those whose primary goal is to terrorize in the name of Allah? How do such people dismiss the reality of murderous attacks committed against innocents? One wonders what folks of this mindset were thinking on September 12, 2001, or December 8, 1941. Some of my friends are predisposed to cut individuals of this ilk a break, but not me. Their naïveté is especially dangerous in a world where bad guys are able to perpetrate mass casualty events with a modicum of planning and execution.

Not A Warlike Nation

Prosperous, free people abhor war. Democracies do not typically maintain a permanent war footing. A comfortable country does not easily send its sons and daughters to fight in faraway places. It is no surprise that such a country and culture could become lazy—even withdrawn—in the absence of an organized, direct threat. Witness America's periodic flirtation with isolationism in the aftermath of two world wars. (This was what Churchill warned Britain and the free world about in the early 1930s.) Witness, also, the wildly enthusiastic audience reaction whenever Representative Ron Paul, and now his son, Kentucky Senator Rand Paul, bemoan US interventionism abroad at GOP presidential debates and rallies. When a seemingly endless, lower profile war with daily casualty reports is added to the mix, it makes for a generalized public disillusionment. And such was the case in 2012, as public opinion polls showed a majority of Americans wished to disengage from Afghanistan as quickly as possible. Decisions based on unstable public opinion are ill advised, however. Historically, they do not survive troubling, but temporary, political exigencies. Had we made decisions about the Iraqi War based on such, the war would have been terminated too early, perhaps, by popular demand before the successful "surge" resulted in a legitimate claim of "mission accomplished."

Nevertheless, public opinion does count, particularly where reports from the front regularly bring troubling news. This is why I have serious doubts about America's ability to sustain a long-running (albeit situational) offensive in the terror war. The American public is rightfully frustrated with an inept post-war occupation of Iraq and a haltingly successfully, drawn out disengagement in Afghanistan. Both experiences serve as painful reminders about the dangers inherent in nation building (once a popular GOP talking point during the Clinton era), particularly where the countries at issue are balkanized and prone to tribal or sectarian violence.

America's post 9/11 foreign adventures are demonstrably different from the divisive experience of Vietnam. That Cold War era conflict was brought home in the form of an anti-war movement born of battlefield casualties inflicted in Southeast Asia, not the streets of lower Manhattan. Vietnam's lessons about the serial difficulties attendant to guerilla warfare and the public opinion impact of daily casualty counts are not lost on Americans of a certain age, however. And it was this influential group of voters who gradually became disenchanted with America's two Bush era wars.

U.S. Resolve and National Identity

So what circumstance does it take to sustain American public support for foreign military engagements going forward? This is a difficult question given our recent experience with wars of limited duration and purpose. Nevertheless, a compelling national security rationale, measureable competence to get the job done, and quantifiable progress seem to be the minimum asking price for entry into a shooting war. Such is the primary vestige of our Vietnam learning experience. *Compelling* in this context means such engagements be of generally agreed upon necessity, and not of choice. Any venture begun *or* then conducted without these essential elements will most assuredly lose public support at a rapid pace. Political support will quickly follow suit, regardless of the degree of traumatic event that triggered the conflict in the first place.

The Peace Lover's Challenge

America's ability to sustain difficult, long-term security commitments is inexorably linked to our national identity. It's all about how we view ourselves, and our role in the world going forward. Will we continue our leadership in dangerous times, or do we wish to emulate the slow but steady decline of Europe's great democracies?

Certainly, our recent determination to over-engineer our economy, borrow against future generations, and further enlarge our already huge welfare state reflects a preference for the latter. So does an Obama-era inclination to accelerate our military downsizing. The numbers in this regard are startling: proposed cuts in carrier strength, the F-35 Joint Strike fighter, and Army and Marine downsizing mark a significant divestment of our ability to project American military might around the world.

Periodic, limited wars of varied success have led to this historically dangerous path. Indeed, the public's decidedly mixed opinions about foreign entanglements over the last forty years (including foreign aid) leads to a politically perilous place as our friends *and enemies* remain confused about what course America will follow, and if America possesses the required staying power once things get dicey on the ground. Mixed signals from a viscerally anti-war Obama administration only add to the confusion.

Some believe a post-Afghanistan drawdown will be a tonic for what ails our sputtering economy. They see a peace dividend in the form of available cash no longer diverted to two expensive wars. It's a new paradigm —defense on the cheap, a ready-made mantra for a war weary, debt-laden nation looking for some sign of fiscal sanity from Washington, D.C. A "low-cost" and "small footprint" approach clearly carries an Obama administration imprint. Of course, a peace dividend in the hands of progressives simply results in lots more *domestic* spending—and lots more government.

It can also deepen a predisposition toward placating despots and other miscreant world leaders. The thought process is easy to follow: the world sure looks safer (and less in need of expensive American military engagement) where you truly believe the Russian bear can be charmed into friendlier "reset" mode, the Muslim Brotherhood demonstrates moderation in temperament and deed, and the ayatollahs in Iran are responsive to western calls for scaling back their nuclear ambitions.

That the reflexively dovish Obama buys into this indulgent mindset is a matter of fact. Recall the 2008 campaign pledge to sit down with hostile leaders "without precondition" or the 2009 world apology tour of major Muslim countries. It's Psych 101: the President wants to believe in the benefits of his outreach campaign so much that he clings to his talking points, despite overwhelming evidence to the contrary.

Obama's Dilemma

Rarely does the world of public affairs allow us insight into how an anti-war progressive responds when confronted with the reality of enormous political power. But such an instructional (and disturbing) example is brought to us by the twice-elected administration of Barack Hussein Obama.

On the plus side, so much of the progressive indictment of Bush era terror policies (rendition, detention, drone warfare, Gitmo) has been forgotten. The reflexively indulgent anti-war progressive could not pull the trigger on these policies (excuse the pun) when confronted with the realities of a post 9/11 presidency. What sounded good on the campaign trail and in front of anti-war, student audiences just would not fly once the seriousness of the security threat became a part of the daily briefing schedule—all to the good in the interest of keeping America safe. That the leaders of the anti-war movement have by-and-large been silent during this "Obama 180" speaks far more to their hatred of George Bush than their principled opposition to America's conduct in the war on terror. Henceforth, their selectively militant attitudes should be viewed in a more political context; they get far less excited about civil liberties when it's one of their own in charge of a shooting war.

Yet, observers and pundits of all stripes have not missed the essential unease with which the President approaches his Commander in Chief duties. Indeed, Chicago-style "community activist" and "Commander of the United States Marine Corps" rarely appear on the same resume. Accordingly, an aggressive use of his considerable military architecture is counter-intuitive for the anti-war activist. This discomfort presents itself in a decidedly disjointed foreign policy platform:

ISRAEL: A stated wish to create "space" between America and Israel, followed by a historic and uncomfortable Oval Office dressing down by Prime Minister "Bebe" Netanyahu, followed by a hard rhetorical tilt toward Israel on the heels of the 2012 election (transparent, yet politically effective as the re-election campaign garnered 69% of the Jewish vote). No wonder Netanyahu worries about what a notoriously guarded Obama would do if/when Iran succeeds in securing a nuclear bomb;

EGYPT: A clear distancing from the Mubarak government on the eve of large anti-government protests, followed by aggressive outreach to a Muslim Brotherhood-led Morsi government, followed by tepid criticism of a wildly unpopular, undemocratic Islamist Constitution, followed by less than enthusiastic support for the (anti-Morsi) pro-democracy demonstrators during the summer of 2013;

AFGHANISTAN: A McCain-type military surge fast on the heels of a promise to withdraw our troops by a certain date, followed up with few and far between reports of progress but plenty of declarations about America's intent to leave the premises—on schedule;

LIBYA: An unwillingness to assist the Libyan rebels (even on humanitarian grounds) followed by a last minute decision to join an anti-Saddam Hussein, European-led coalition followed by little of consequence until a sitting American Ambassador was murdered at our Consulate in Benghazi, followed by a series of high profile misrepresentations (to be kind) about the cause of the terrorist attacks, followed by (embarrassed) silence and a stated desire to put the entire episode behind us. For anyone wishing to take issue with this statement of facts, recall the incriminating retrospective of former Secretary of State Hillary Clinton (in a decidedly defensive appearance before Congress) once the administration's "Muslim video" line had been exposed as phony: "After all, what does it matter?";

SYRIA: A stated policy of non-intervention (even when the anti-Assad rebels included decidedly pro-Western elements) during the initial stages of Assad's murderous campaign against anti-government rebels, followed by a promise to arm the rebels should Assad be found to have used weapons of mass destruction (WMD) ("a line in the sand"), followed by a claim that real evidence of WMD had not been produced despite the fact that our western allies had confirmed their use, followed by an announcement (by a deputy national security advisor) that the U.S. would sparingly arm the rebels; followed by assurances to Assad and Putin that any U.S. military response would be limited and not intended to achieve regime change in one of the world's most notorious dictatorships;

RUSSIA: A Hillary Clinton initiated "reset" intended to distance the accommodating Obama Administration from the "cowboy" Bush together with a (Russian requested) broken promise to Poland to station defensive missiles in that pro-Western country, followed by relentless pokes in the eye, from UN vetos to Julian Assange to an aggressive and provocative support of the Assad regime;

DRONES: A major foreign policy address highlighting the President's hyper-aggressive drone campaign in Afghanistan and Pakistan (far beyond Bush administration efforts) while admitting to the targeted killing of four American terrorists and an unknown number of collateral victims, but almost immediately followed with a highly promoted War on Terror "reset" speech wherein the President signaled further American disengagement now that al-Qaeda was "on the path to defeat"—a dubious proposition, more campaign slogan than fact, but most assuredly a notion the administration wishes to perpetuate in the public consciousness.

In addition to these often incoherent policy flip-flops, there has been the administration's insistence on rather goofy reinventions of familiar terms and concepts, all in order to create a more benign dialogue with hostile regimes. Hence, terrorism morphed into "man-caused disasters," a murderous act of religiously driven terror at Fort Hood was identified as "workplace violence," and foreign military engagements became "overseas contingency operations."

Domestic Surveillance

The President's "rather not think about it" mindset also extends to the considerable uproar over the National Security Agency's domestic surveillance practices. But the domestic context makes it even more uncomfortable for the civil liberties-friendly former law school professor. Accordingly, the message to his progressive base has been a familiar one: "don't blame me; I'm simply the inheritor of all these problematic security programs from that out-of-control cowboy George Bush" (a practiced and perfected Obama tactic). A related ploy is to assume observer status pursuant to his former professional role ("I welcome the national debate over security versus freedom") as if he was overseeing a moot court competition at Harvard.

Whether a substantive debate regarding NSA surveillance programs will break out in 2014 or 2016 is anyone's guess, but the detached, moot court-like analysis is meant to distance the administration from a public relations mess while buying time to get over an uneasy, watchful response from mainstream America. The strategy may indeed succeed; the left leaning media regularly cuts the guy a break whenever he takes leave from leftist orthodoxy. As for the rest of us, the country should not hold its collective breath waiting for this President to lead a national debate on the merits of domestic surveillance practices in a post-9/11 world. It's just a bit too far outside his comfort zone.

The constant theme here is leading from behind; allowing world events (and those opposed to U.S. strategic interests) to dictate the terms and tenor of U.S. engagements, because (although he engages once in awhile) he's just not comfortable asserting American might around the world.

Such a worldview carries real strategic costs, including the denigration of our ability to impose our will or, at a minimum, influence events in dangerous places. It also calls into question a vital element of our national identity, a heretofore Kennedy-esque identity aggressively engaged in furthering the cause of freedom—an identity that up until now had pride in our ability to engage and defeat bad guys *away* from American soil.

Making the Public Case

So, herein lies the great challenge for American national security going forward. It's not so much the number of Marine divisions to field or Navy ships to build. Those policy decisions ebb and flow along with the philosophical leanings of presidents, party control of Congress, and large budget deals. Here, peace dividends and military build-ups alike have limited shelf lives. But it is the elements necessary to justify American sacrifice in faraway places that presents the true challenge for an increasingly leery public. Today's public seems to require some type of Congressional blessing combined with a clearly defined mission and definition of success. An added component in this social media era would be a transparency needed to sustain public support and rebut domestic opposition as real-time communications drive our news cycle.

Various iterations of this multi-pronged "intervention doctrine" have been floated since Vietnam. Leaders of both political parties would do well to think long and hard about following one before young Americans are again asked to place themselves in harm's way on the next front in the modern terror war.

| NATIONAL SECURITY
AND OUR NATIONAL IDENTITY
CHAPTER FOOTNOTES |

1. Alison Mitchell, "Clinton Offers Challenge To Nation, Declaring 'The Era of Big Government is Over'," *The New York Times,* January 24, 1996.
2. It should be noted in this complex search for evidence that there is disquieting evidence from the FBI's George Piro's interviews with Saddam Hussein that plans for such weapons development may have lay in waiting in a surviving Saddam polity. "Interrogator Shares Saddam's Confessions," CBS News, February 11, 2009.
3. U.S. Army Center for Military History, "Still No Exact Figure for D-Day Dead," Fox News, June 4, 2004.

SECURING A HEALTHCARE *AGENDA*, NOT QUALITY HEALTHCARE

"... if I were starting from scratch, if we didn't have a system in which employers had typically provided health care, I would probably go with a single-payer system."

—BARACK OBAMA,
Democratic debate on CNN, Myrtle Beach, South Carolina,
January 22, 2008

There has been one critical missing element within the great American healthcare debate: *honesty*. As a result, the American people have been left with the most damaging single piece of federal legislation in recent memory, representing one of the most significant missed opportunities of our generation. All sides are complicit in the creation of this mess, and our healthcare delivery system has continued to hemorrhage as a result.

Plain truths are often forgotten or covered up: the system is too expensive, an inordinate amount of money is expended during the last few months of life, there is far too much litigation growing out of poor (but not necessarily negligent) results, too many high risk specialists are choosing to retire or teach rather than pay outrageous malpractice premiums, and the increasingly complex matrix of insurance coverage and accompanying paperwork makes the system too complicated for the average patient.

Yet, transparent and clear truths about how we got here and what we need to do in order to dig ourselves out of the ditch remain in short supply. Recent experience with the *Patient Protection and Affordable Care Act* (otherwise known as Obamacare) speaks to the enormity of the problem. This arcane, multi-layered plunge into supposedly fundamental reform has generated countless instances of over-selling, mind-bending naïveté, or worse. Major elements of the bill have already proven to be unworkable, prohibitively expensive, overly complex, and a political liability for the Obama administration. Indeed, dire warnings about an Obamacare-generated "huge train wreck" began shortly after the President was sworn in for a second term. Unsurprisingly, pleas for "more resources" (Washington-speak for additional tax dollars) were offered as the only solution for what ails proper implementation of the healthcare law.[1] And the most negative impacts are not scheduled for implementation until 2016, a standard Washington tactic when it comes to paying a tab we cannot afford. It's all so familiar: politicians performing a legislative hit-and-run, leaving a mess for future politicians to clean up.

The saga surrounding the implementation of Obamacare may be a continuing nightmare in practice, but it had one beneficial impact: the accompanying national debate served to sharpen public opinion about the problems that require repair within our increasingly complex healthcare delivery system. Such is the byproduct of a multi-year campaign to reconfigure nearly 20 percent of the US economy. Indeed, the President's fixation on delivering the centerpiece of his 2008 campaign platform required the media to focus on the major cost and quality of care drivers within our hybrid system. The mass media performed this function well enough over an extended timeframe, but could not be expected to fully illuminate the myriad complexities contained within two bills (*The Patient Protection and Affordable Care Act* and *The Health Care and Education Reconciliation Act*) that total 961 pages.[2] In fact, a majority of the most important "reviewers" —the 535 Members of Congress who were required to vote on the bill—lacked the time, energy, and/or interest to read the legislative monstrosity. The intellectual (and practical) dilemma was summed up by House Speaker Nancy Pelosi's plea in the days prior to the final vote: "We have to pass the bill so that you can find out what is in it." What was one of the few truisms to escape from the Speaker's mouth has become just one of many indictments issued by political opponents and pundits alike. A veto-proof Democratic Congress may have served as a temporary barrier to general outrage, but outrage nevertheless took hold as the public at large began to decipher the many dangerous tentacles of the bill.

Unsurprisingly, the adverse reaction only gathered additional steam in the run-up to the 2010 midterm elections, wherein so many of the promises made during extended Congressional debate were proven dubious at best, outright misrepresentations at worst. The most damning aspect of the entire episode occurred when not a single Democrat in a competitive race ran on an Obamacare platform. Politics is known to be a lonely profession, but this wholesale repudiation of the sitting President's signature legislative accomplishment stood alone. Alas, most Democratic hopefuls could not run fast enough, as the GOP rang up historic gains on an anti-Obamacare platform. The Obama White House certainly got the message: a remarkable de-emphasis accompanied the historic legislative accomplishment during the presidential campaign of 2012, including the mini-honeymoon period following the Supreme Court's blessing of the individual mandate.

A bit of historical perspective is in order. The gut wrenching healthcare debate of 2009-2012 was merely the latest (albeit the most acrimonious) installment of a long-running healthcare saga within American politics. The great debates of late surround monumental policy initiatives such as Medicare, Medicaid, managed care, and Medicare Part D. These and other policy milestones were accompanied by the now familiar philosophical firestorms concerning government's responsibility to its people—and an individual's responsibility to himself.

The politically poisonous atmosphere that accompanied the Obamacare debate marked a high water point in this long running ideological battle. The legislation's attempt to expand government control over such a significant percentage of the American economy represented a major leap forward for the proponents of government generated and government subsidized medical care. That it received Congressional approval from only one party reflected the depth of the ideological divide and the seriousness of the partisan opposition. Indeed, one is hard pressed to recall any such dramatic change in national policy which included *uniform* opposition from the minority party. In retrospect, the deep political thinkers within the Obama White House should not have been surprised by 2010's grassroots repudiation; instead, they should have fully expected the voter discontent that removed Pelosi from the Speaker's Chair and left Harry Reid with a razor-thin majority in the US Senate.

Facts and Fiction

My most effective applause line during Campaign 2010 was a mocking dig at the complexities of Obamacare: "I'm no longer a Member of Congress . . . so I *have* read the bill." The line would typically be followed by a brief pause, and then a knowing giggle (if not an out and out laugh) by the assembled who suspected that most Members of Congress possessed only a passing notion into the substance of the Affordable Care Act. In fact, my eight-year tenure in the House provided excellent perspective on what the typical Member knew (and did not know) about the bill's constantly changing provisions.

My (informed) suspicion: the vast majority of Members were both familiar with the major policy provisions contained in the original draft and reliant on committee staff and/or party caucus to produce the daily talking points that in reality represented the Member's major source of knowledge. Few, if any, possessed the time or inclination to study the many policy changes instituted throughout the legislative process. One unfair critique emanated from the right, where conservative radio talk show hosts raised the expectation that each Member of Congress should have read the bill and amendments in their entirety, in addition to the other bills presented to Members in subcommittee, full committee, and on the Floor on a daily basis. Of course, such expectations are unrealistic given the fact that most Members are not speed-readers and have other time consuming duties. Nevertheless, I knew that the majority of Members remained too reliant on the aforementioned daily talking points, and that still others were unfamiliar with the many intricate policy changes that would soon prove to have profound (and negative) impact in the real world of patients and physicians.

The most efficient way to interpret the myriad policy determinations contained within Obamacare is to deconstruct the bill into its essential elements, outlining the major policy changes that will have such a dramatic impact on our collective quality of life going forward. Understanding these key elements will also help to provide direction on where health policy should proceed if our country wishes to reestablish itself as a world leader in healthcare delivery, cost effectiveness, and consumer satisfaction.

Obamacare Points to Consider

Truly vital policy calls remain, to some extent, in the eye of the beholder, but most observers would agree that seven major policy determinations within Obamacare reflect a hard left turn in national health policy. In effect, these policy decisions represent a historic shift away from a market-orientated, choice paradigm to a government sponsored and controlled paradigm—just the type of result promised by freshman Senator Barack Obama on the 2008 campaign trail. So, what precisely are the elite seven? And how do they serve to undermine what has heretofore been a system biased toward employer provided benefits and patient choice?

A Regulatory Nightmare

Obamacare encompasses more than 700 individual directives to various federal agencies, most of them targeted to the Department of Health & Human Services (HHS).[3] The most telling feature of this regulatory nightmare: during its first two years of life, the law spawned 2.8 million words (Americans for Limited Government Research Foundation describes the volume as three and one-half times the size of the Bible, 5.1 times the length of War and Peace, and 620 times the length of the U.S. Constitution) of regulatory interpretation with many more millions to come.[4] One of the most widely reported, early examples of regulatory overkill pertained to the six pages Obamacare devoted to the mostly unfamiliar vehicle known as an *Accountable Care Organization*, which HHS turned into a 127-page proposed regulation in short order.[5]

Possibly the most well known and controversial Obamacare regulation concerned the HHS rule that religious schools, charities, and hospitals would no longer be exempt from providing contraceptive services to their employees under what is generally known as the "Conscience Clause exception" for religious affiliated organizations.

No issue generates more emotion than a woman's right to choose. But most abortion-related votes today pertain to one or more collateral issues rather than the legal right to the procedure. Indeed, intense emotional debates since *Roe vs. Wade* have produced a unique lexicon, as legislators regularly debate the merits and implications of "judicial bypass," "parental consent," "partial birth," and the many complexities attendant to Medicaid (taxpayer) funding under certain circumstances.

The Conscience Clause

What was never an issue, even in the hyper-progressive and overwhelmingly pro-choice Maryland legislature, was the guarantee of Conscience Clause protection. The notion that religious employers would not be forced to provide abortion or other contraceptive services in contravention of their religious beliefs was the third rail of abortion politics. Similar recognition of conscience exemption was the norm in state legislatures around the country. Like it or not, even the most ardent pro-choice legislators accepted conscience provisions as part of any statutory regime. That is, until the secular progressives within the Obama administration reversed this bipartisan embrace by requiring all health insurance plans to cover contraception and sterilization services, including some services that many view as tantamount to abortion.

That major Catholics within the Obama administration (particularly Vice President Biden and former Chief of Staff Daly) raised strong objection appears from all accounts to be accurate. Besides the seemingly bad politics, these two gentlemen may have recalled the President's circa 2009 pledge at Notre Dame that the pro-life views of Catholics would be honored by his administration, and not tinkered with in the interest of healthcare reform. (In retrospect, the intended beneficiaries of the President's remarks should have been more skeptical of such assurances in light of Obama's strong pro-choice views and voting history.) Unfortunately, however, Messrs Biden and Daly lost the internal debate: Valerie Jarrett and other like-minded liberals within the administration carried the day. Indeed, such a rare opportunity to overturn one of pro-life's foundational principles could not be ignored.

Fierce reaction from the Catholic Church and other mainstream denominations moved the administration to offer (almost) immediate, if unsatisfactory, compromise by extending the exemption to religious groups that employ members of their own religion, i.e., churches. Obama's Department of Health and Human Services further negotiated a provision that would have insurance companies shoulder the mandate rather than the religious employer—not such a good deal for an institution (such as Notre Dame) that self-insures. And even a re-elected Obama administration offered additional concessions that sought to expand the definition of religious (employer) groups to include affiliated non-profit organizations and "house[s] of worship" that employ "persons of different religious faiths."[6]

In the heat of Campaign 2012, however, Obama's initial moves to mitigate reaction within religious America gained little traction. That is until, in a stroke of political good fortune, former Pennsylvania Senator Rick Santorum's conservative views on contraception took the conscience story off page one. Talk about fortuitous timing: Santorum's campaign comment concerning "the dangers of contraception"[7] opened the door for the Democratic Party to dust off its "Republicans are anti-women" mantra. Seems that every four years Republican presidential candidates must respond to this time tested charge. A persistent GOP gender gap with women reflects a less than successful history in this regard, a problem that was further illustrated by the Romney campaign's rather miserable performance (an 11 point loss) with members of the fairer sex.

All political campaigns must end, however. Senator Santorum officially called it quits on April 10, 2012. And a mere six weeks later, 43 Catholic groups, including Notre Dame and the Archdioceses of New York and Washington, sued the administration over its heavy-handed intrusion into the conscience clause, and religious liberty.

There are a few Obamacare reminders with respect to religious liberty one must remember. First, even in the absence of Obamacare, every private employer in America, including faith-based employers, was free to offer unlimited contraception services within their employer plans. Secondly, the administration's regulation was always about mandating which medical services employers must include in their employee health care plans, despite instances where an employer's religious convictions are to the contrary. Finally, the administration's compromise exemption is quite limited: all employers who serve people regardless of religious affiliation will be forced by the federal government to provide contraception, sterilization, and morning-after pill coverage to their employees. In other words, churches are exempt, but faith-based affiliated institutions such as hospitals, clinics, colleges, adoption agencies, and food pantries are not. A second federal mandate: such services will be offered free of charge by private insurance companies.

The crux of this matter is clear to all who wish to see: religious freedom under the First Amendment will be so narrowly drawn that many previously exempt religiously affiliated employers will now be subjected to Obamacare's contraception mandate. Father John Jenkins, President of the University of Notre Dame, captured the Catholic Church's view of the onerous Obamacare compromise:

> Many of our faculty, staff and students—both Catholic and non-Catholic—have made conscientious decisions to use contraceptives. As we assert the right to follow our conscience, we respect their right to follow theirs. And we believe that, if the Government wishes to provide such services, means are available that do not compel religious organizations to serve as its agents . . . We do not seek to impose our religious beliefs on others; we simply ask that the Government not impose its values on the University when those values conflict with our religious teachings.[8]

I was reminded of President Jenkins' request as I read the December 19, 2012 headline in *The Daily Caller*: "Will Obamacare Drive the Little Sisters of the Poor Out of the United States?"

Yes, the beloved order of nuns that runs nursing homes for the aged and infirm was forced to consider leaving the United States. You see, the Order's policy of hiring employees without regard to religious affiliation falls outside Obamacare's more limited conscience clause, requiring the Sisters to offer insurance services (contraception, sterilization, abortion) they find objectionable. Their resulting dilemma: either violate strongly held religious doctrine or leave their mission in America. Strike one for extreme feminism, and against common sense. And 50 percent of Catholics voted for this guy?

The President's more partisan defenders contend the conscience clause debate is about a woman's right to secure the contraception option of her choice, but in reality it is to guarantee continued younger female support for the President and Democratic candidates. They also understand the dire political consequences should the issue be viewed instead through the prism of religious freedom.

Individual freedom is the primary victim under the myriad mandates of Obamacare, and nowhere is this loss of freedom more pronounced than under the new and not-so-improved conscience clause exemption. Should a subsequent Congress repeal or defund Obamacare, (remember Speaker Boehner and a pro-conscience clause majority still control the chamber where spending bills originate) any new healthcare package should leave the well-established conscience protection alone. Health reform is difficult enough without (gratuitously) chipping away at this cornerstone of religious liberty.

It is impossible to predict the nature and extent of the regulatory burden represented by a fully implemented Obamacare. One outcome is acknowledged by all sides, however: many of the important decisions will not be made by the democratically elected representatives of the people. Instead, they will be issued by an army of unelected, unaccountable regulators. Such is the legacy of the Obama administrative state. This Administration inherited a gigantic government and made it bigger, stronger, and more intrusive. But its power is derived from its permanency. The old cliché applies: politicians may come and go, but the bureaucracy lives forever. And the newly empowered Obama bureaucracy enjoys a degree of power over the personal decision making authority of ordinary people never before seen in our history.

Think You Can Keep What You Have?
Think Again.

Obamacare sanctions (fines) employers with 50 or more employees who do not offer health insurance to their workforce. It's a revenue raiser intended to cover the ever-escalating costs of the bill. But one of the great unknowns generated by the law goes to the heart of healthcare choice: the notion that increased employer costs and regulatory burdens would cause large employers to simply pay fines (and dump their newly insurance-deprived employees on state or federally run exchanges) *rather* than continue to offer employer subsidized insurance. The fact that some of the largest American employers would consider such a move has caused plenty of Democratic heartburn. In one dramatic scenario, AT&T estimated that its healthcare costs would drop from $2.4 billion to $600 million if the company simply dropped employee coverage and paid the government-mandated fine instead.[9]

A 2011 analysis by McKinsey & Company confirms what so many economists not employed by the Obama administration had predicted all along: Obamacare will cause a dramatic decrease in the number of employers who offer health insurance to their employees.[10] A McKinsey analyst observed that such a change would impact "something in the range of 80 to 100 million individuals."[11] So much for the oft-cited Congressional Budget Office report that estimated only about eight or nine million workers would lose their employer based coverage and end up in government subsidized insurance.[12] Even the mathematically challenged can figure out the draconian consequences for the federal budget: millions of new entrants into government subsidized coverage (government subsidies under Obamacare run to $88,000 a year for families) mean billions of additional Obamacare generated costs.

McKinsey et al. was further backed up in an April 2013 Senate Finance Committee hearing led by Chairman Max Baucas, Montana Democrat and primary sponsor of Obamacare.

The topic was Obamacare oversight, and the assembled received an earful from the business community. Most importantly, testimony from numerous large employers confirmed the worst suspicions of Obamacare opponents: many of America's larger businesses will pay a fee rather than continue employer-based coverage, many are converting some of their full-time employees to part-time status in order to avoid Obamacare mandates, and many employees who had lost health benefits were experiencing great difficulty in signing up for state healthcare exchanges. It seems the IRS computers experience glitches when asked to match up with health exchange computers. The result: millions potentially sentenced to a "no health care twilight zone." Note that these are the same folks who had enjoyed high levels of satisfaction with their previous employer based coverage. A further bit of testimony added insult to injury; it appears that Obamacare's considerable subsidies are not generous enough to match the same level of coverage enjoyed under the now eliminated employer based plans.

Such serious problems led to the surprise announcement(s) that the administration intended to suspend enforcement of the employer mandate for a year and follow an "honor system" in calculating eligibility for exchange coverage and the subsidies that will often accompany the new coverage.

In reality, the move simply delayed implementation of the considerable data collection requirements (employee personal information and information relating to those who are eligible but decline coverage) including the cost of the coverage and salary of the employee.[13]

The country must now wait for the rest of employer-America to complete their internal cost-benefit calculations during the run-up to full implementation of Obamacare, whenever that may occur. In the interim, the daunting notion of large employers willingly breaking the back of the nation's employer-based healthcare system is causing many sleepless nights in Washington, D.C. Remember a certain pledge to the effect that those Americans happy with their healthcare would be able to keep their coverage? This pledge was joined with a promise to protect our long established employer based system of health insurance. Both assurances became a familiar mantra during the often-ugly national debate over Obamacare and were repeated by President Obama. Both now look to be considerably less than accurate. Unless, of course, one is fortunate enough to enjoy a membership in a certain labor union, particularly those possessing a proclivity toward supporting that same Obama fellow in his campaign for a second term.

Indeed, the Obama administration had granted 1,472 "waivers of participation" as of July 2011.[14] Labor unions received fully 50 percent of the administration's largess, a revealing fact given organized labor's professed enthusiasm for the legislation. Two further anomalies: in April 2011 nearly 20 percent of the total waivers approved were for former House Speaker Nancy Pelosi's district, while Senate Majority Leader Harry Reid secured a waiver for all insurers operating in the individual market in the entire state of Nevada.[15] The Obama administration's rationale for exempting an entire state: Obamacare "might lead to the destabilization of the individual market."[16]

But a series of temporary waivers was not enough to pacify organized labor in the longer term. Union disillusionment with Obamacare gathered additional (and seemingly permanent) momentum in the early days of Obama II, as prominent labor groups began to focus on the reality of increased healthcare premiums and work-week issues on behalf of their members. Specifically, union leadership rebelled at the prospect of union members in employer-sponsored plans being declared ineligible for subsidies available to those forced to enter an exchange. The classic big labor response? Ask the taxpayer to subsidize premiums for lower income workers covered by employer-sponsored plans.[17] Or, the route exposed by the (previously pro-Obamacare) United Union of Roofers, who called for repeal or complete reform of The Affordable Care Act in April of 2013. The Union minced no words in their public statement: "[the bill is] inconsistent with the promise that those who were satisfied with their employer-sponsored coverage could keep it."[18] It all came to a head in the summer of 2013 as the leaders of three major unions issued a very public challenge (complete with the usual political quid-pro-quo) to Harry Reid and Nancy Pelosi. The letter read as follows:

Dear Leader Reid and Leader Pelosi:

When you and the President sought our support for the Affordable Care Act (ACA), you pledged that if we liked the health plans we have now, we could keep them. Sadly, that promise is under threat. Right now, unless you and the Obama administration enact an equitable fix, the ACA will shatter not only our hard-earned health benefits, but destroy the foundation of the 40 hour work week that is the backbone of the American middle class.

Like millions of other Americans, our members are front-line workers in the American economy. We have been strong supporters of the notion that all Americans should have access to quality, affordable health care. We have also been strong supporters of you. In campaign after campaign we have put boots on the ground, gone door-to-door to get out the vote, run phone banks and raised money to secure this vision.

Now this vision has come back to haunt us.

Since the ACA was enacted, we have been bringing our deep concerns to the administration, seeking reasonable regulatory interpretations to the statute that would help prevent the destruction of non-profit health plans. As you both know first-hand, our persuasive arguments have been disregarded and met with a stone wall by the White House and the pertinent agencies. This is especially stinging because other stakeholders have repeatedly received successful interpretations for their respective grievances. Most disconcerting of course is last week's huge accommodation for the employer community—extending the statutorily mandated "December 31, 2013" deadline for the employer mandate and penalties.

Time is running out: Congress wrote this law; we voted for you. We have a problem; you need to fix it. The unintended consequences of the ACA are severe. Perverse incentives are already creating nightmare scenarios:

First, the law creates an incentive for employers to keep employees' work hours below 30 hours a week. Numerous employers have begun to cut workers' hours to avoid this obligation, and many of them are doing so openly. The impact is two-fold: fewer hours means less pay while also losing our current health benefits. Second, millions of Americans are covered by non-profit health insurance plans like the ones in which most of our members participate. These non-profit plans are governed jointly by unions and companies under the Taft-Hartley Act. Our health plans have been built over decades by working men and women. Under the ACA as interpreted by the Administration, our employees will be treated differently and not be

*eligible for subsidies afforded other citizens. As such, many em-
ployees will be relegated to second-class status and shut out of
the help the law offers to for-profit insurance plans.*

*And finally, even though non-profit plans like ours won't
receive the same subsidies as for-profit plans, they'll be taxed
to pay for those subsidies. Taken together, these restrictions
will make non-profit plans like ours unsustainable, and will
undermine the health-care market of viable alternatives to the
big health insurance companies.*

*On behalf of the millions of working men and women we
represent and the families they support, we can no longer
stand silent in the face of elements of the Affordable Care Act
that will destroy the very health and wellbeing of our members
along with millions of other hardworking Americans.*

*We believe that there are commonsense corrections that can
be made within the existing statute that will allow our members to continue to keep their current health plans and benefits just as you and the President pledged. Unless changes are
made, however, that promise is hollow.*

*We continue to stand behind real health care reform, but
the law as it stands will hurt millions of Americans including
the members of our respective unions.*

We are looking to you to make sure these changes are made.

*James P. Hoffa, General President
International Brotherhood of Teamsters*

Joseph Hansen, International President UFCW

D. Taylor, President UNITE-HERE[19]

This very public dressing down was soon followed by an
equally aggressive letter writing campaign from the National

Treasury Employees Union— the union that includes the same IRS employees charged with implementing Obamacare—asking to be exempted from the Obamacare exchanges.[20] Such irony must not be lost on those of us who opposed the bill from its inception.

Obamacare and Progressivism

The proliferation of waivers and demand for additional subsidies under Obamacare reflects a recurring theme within progressivism itself: it's all about what it says, not what it does. Think about it; the progressive left regularly issues pronouncements intended to capture the moral high ground, yet only proves to be a "renter" in most cases. Indeed, it seems that when it comes to life's major decisions, the left is far more enthusiastic about how it feels as opposed to what it does. A sampling of progressive selectivity:

- Progressives profess their love of public education but send their kids to private schools;
- Progressives profess to love low-cost public housing, just not in their neighborhoods;
- Progressives profess to love the poor, but tend to live amongst the rich;
- Progressives profess to love gun control, but buy weapons in bulk when threatened; and
- Progressives profess to love socialized medicine, so long as it does not apply to them.

This last item captures the essential contradiction of Obamacare. What more powerful indictment than the selective awarding of waivers to the privileged few?

The Infamous IPAB

Another example of Obamacare's anti-choice agenda is the well analyzed *Independent Payment Advisory Board* (IPAB). Scheduled to begin its deliberations in 2014, the fifteen-member appointed panel is tasked with the enormously important job of selecting the procedures, drugs, and reimbursement rates to be covered by Medicare. Although infamously and perhaps somewhat exaggeratedly labeled a "death panel" by the likes of Sarah Palin and others, its core charter is to save money through healthcare rationing—a task to be accomplished by an *unelected* commission.

Opposition to the IPAB has been wide and deep, not to mention left and right. Indeed, well-known liberals such as Rep. Loretta Sanchez (D - CA), Rep. Chaka Fattah (D - PA), former Vermont Governor and Chairman of the Democratic National Committee Howard Dean, and former Representatives Pete Stark (D - CA) and Barney Frank (D - MA) have publicly repudiated the notion of an appointed board possessing such extraordinary power.[21] Further, IPAB's future was not helped with the Congressional Budget Office's projection that it would not save a penny before 2021.[22] A likely future result: should certain provisions of Obamacare fail to survive the Congressional amendment process and periodic defunding efforts, this bad idea will likely be one of them. Nevertheless, it is ironic that an administration so practiced in the fine art of "Medi-scare" would find itself so vulnerable to attack by some of its closest political allies.

• • •

The Individual Mandate

Of course, the most controversial Obamacare provision is the individual mandate, which requires all US citizens to purchase health insurance or face a "tax," a burden Chief Justice Roberts found to pass Constitutional muster. Here, choice is taken away from individual Americans. For the first time in American history, the federal government will now require every adult to purchase a commercial product. This new federal mandate is the cornerstone of Obamacare; without it, the large cost savings that will (allegedly) follow from its implementation would be impossible to attain, even on paper.

The lead-up to the mandate's arrival at the high court was anything but boring, as 26 states and the *National Federation of Independent Business* filed lawsuits against Obamacare, while Virginia, Liberty University, and the Thomas Moore Law Center filed separate actions to overturn the mandate. Voters in Ohio and Missouri approved referendums against the mandate, while Virginia enacted a law that protects its citizens against "any penalty, assessment, fee, or fine, as a result of his failure to procure or obtain health insurance coverage."[23] Interestingly, a majority of Virginia House Democrats and Black Caucus members backed the measure.[24]

Despite Obamacare's considerable political difficulties, the administration and its left wing allies held out hope that the Court's conservative majority would lose the usually reliable Justice Antonin Scalia, pointing to Scalia's sometimes expansive view of the commerce clause as expressed in a widely analyzed 2006 opinion.[25] Ultimately, no such view of the commerce clause would generate the required five votes, as the five Republican nominated justices made clear their disdain for the administration's preferred interpretation.

How ironic then that the usually reliable Chief Justice Roberts would find an alternative route to rescue the bill. In simple terms, what the Chief Justice gives . . . he also takes away: "The federal government does not have the power to order people to buy health insurance. The federal government does have the power to impose a tax on those without health insurance."[26]

And all of this on the heels of the President's solemn promise that the individual mandate was never to be interpreted as a tax. Talk about winning the battle but losing the war!

One Big Tax Increase

Obamacare's individual mandate and its likely negative impact on employer sponsored health plans has generated so much attention that it is easy to forget the 21 other tax increases estimated to cost American taxpayers in excess of $1.058 trillion over the next ten years.[27] Of course, these numbers are mere estimates. History has taught us that revenue estimates for such a length of time are typically understated. (The original estimate was $569.2 billion.) And the political consequences for these often incorrect "guesstimates" are usually negligible; who will recall Obamacare's wildly off the mark estimates of tax burdens two, three, or four years down the road?

All tax increases are not created equal, however. Analysis has focused on those revenue measures that will most likely suppress economic growth:

- An annual fee on health insurance carriers of $101.7 billion
- An increase in payroll tax and investment income for higher income couples and individuals totaling approximately $317.7 billion

- A higher payroll tax on investment income for higher income couples and individuals totaling $317.7 billion
- An annual fee on manufacturers and importers of branded drugs totaling $34.2 billion
- An excise tax on premium health insurance plans totaling $111 billion
- An excise tax on manufacturers and importers of selected medical devices totaling $29.1 billion
- An increase in the adjusted gross income floor on medical expenses from 7.5 percent to 10 percent totaling approximately $18.7 billion [28]

The Medical Device Tax

Unfortunately, minimal analysis has been directed to the special excise tax on medical device manufacturers. Yet, this tariff is one of the most perplexing. Americans live longer and have higher quality lives due to medical innovation. Just think about the new products and procedures brought to market over the past 25 years. Survival rates multiply when innovators do their thing free of undue government interference. One such governmental club is the ability to tax medical innovation. And in the case of Obamacare, the new tax is especially punishing: the tariff will be collected from *gross revenues*, not profits. Accordingly, manufacturers of life saving and life enhancing products will pay the government its money prior to ever making a buck. The likely result will be fewer manufacturers bringing fewer new products to market. One early study concluded that the tax will reduce American medical research and development by $2 billion a year.[29]

More than 800 companies and industry organizations have signed a letter asking Congress to repeal the ill-considered levy.

And the commencement of device tax-related downsizing and facility closings have arrived in distressing volume. Leading manufacturers such as Welch Allyn, Stryker, Boston Scientific, and Medtronic have announced significant layoffs. Total job loss is difficult to estimate, but the Advanced Medical Technology Association believes its members will lose in the neighborhood of 43,000 jobs once the new tax takes effect.[30] The Manhattan Institute projects direct and indirect job loss will approach 146,000.[31]

In essence, the medical device tax represents the grand slam of bad policies: enhanced development cuts, fewer life sustaining inventions, lost jobs, and the migration of manufacturing jobs overseas. Add it all up and it is a mighty bad outcome for American healthcare.

A Paler America

Another of Obamacare's more desperate but less publicized revenue measures is sure to be unpopular in cold weather America: a new federal tanning tax. Yes, the federal government will now invade your tanning bed, to the tune of $1.5 billion.[32] How distressing that your winter glow will be compromised in the interest of balancing Obamacare's books. I wonder what Jefferson would have thought about this beauty!

The influx of new Obamacare-generated revenue into the federal coffers represents a monumental shift of dollars away from an employer-preferred to a government-subsidized healthcare delivery system. On the left, the progressive nature of the new taxes adds to the new program's attractiveness. Talk about a progressive win-win-win: at least $1.058 trillion in new tax revenue generated primarily from the "rich" to finance a dramatically more far reaching healthcare program while the traditional employer based system slowly ebbs away. Adding insult to injury, the President's campaign promises about his healthcare plan not adding "one dime" to the deficit are officially defunct: the Government Accountability Office now estimates Obamacare will likely add $6.2 trillion to the deficit over the next 75 years.[33] Who said Messrs. Obama and Reid and Madame Pelosi don't think *big*? Only one problem: big means big regulation, big exemptions, big taxes, big spending, and a big loss of freedom. It's just a big loser.

Digging Out: Medical Liability Reform

Large and unpredictable medical malpractice increases periodically fuel legal reform debates in legislatures around the country. Congress is not immune to this cyclical syndrome. These occasional "tort reform" upheavals and ever increasing health insurance increases suffered by employers and their employees were the predicate for the great healthcare debate of 2008, wherein first candidate then President Obama parlayed voter concern over escalating healthcare costs with his well demonstrated enthusiasm for massive federal programs into what became Obamacare. Predictably, however, the "comprehensive" solution sold to the American people failed to address a significant driver of healthcare costs in the real world: defensive medicine.

An often-ignored aspect of healthcare reform measures concerns the more arcane but strong cost drivers within the healthcare marketplace. These costs include everything from how physician fees are generated to operating room fees to the huge research and development costs associated with new drug therapies. Simply put, the cost side of the healthcare equation is exceedingly complex. Indeed, entire legal sub-specialties have grown up around intricate issues such as provider reimbursement rates, drug pricing, patent protection, and medical device innovation.

Suffice to say that the intersection of medicine and law, while a growth industry for lawyers, remains generally unknown to the average person.

What is not so complex is the utilization of defensive medicine: a critical, often unaddressed issue, integrally related to the need for tort reform and ever-increasing healthcare costs and prices. The practice is best defined as the use of needless and/or redundant tests ordered by medical providers in an attempt to protect themselves from medical malpractice lawsuits. Alas, even unnecessary tests do not ensure against everyday malpractice claims in our overly litigious society.

The reality of medical negligence litigation is that most of the serious claims settle out of court. Such cases typically pertain to violations of standards of care resulting in real injury or death. These plaintiffs deserve compensation; no thoughtful reformer takes issue with just compensation for seriously injured claimants. As for bad doctors, it is the duty of state medical boards to regulate the practice of medicine, including reprimands, sanctions, and loss of license, where appropriate.

Two classes of cases are at the core of the "med mal" crisis, however. These situations arise where either a non-negligent medical procedure leads to a poor result or a clearly frivolous case of medical malpractice is filed.

The former occurs with frequency but generates little analysis. Nevertheless, our society has arrived at a charitable (if not equitable) conclusion: someone or something will pay regardless of whether negligence took place. Here, malpractice carriers simply pay (settle) the tab for poor medical results, and pass these increased costs on to the physician in the form of higher insurance rates.

An entirely different set of circumstances applies where a clearly frivolous case is filed. Insurance carriers too often jump to settle these mostly minor cases in order to avoid major legal fees. The calculus is simple: the cost of going forward is far greater than a minimal settlement. Here, the attorneys and claimants get paid, and the insurance carrier gets to wipe another claim off its books. The damage for the medical provider is real, however: loss of reputation, increased insurance premiums, and a declining bottom line often result. So is there any wonder why physicians expend so much time and resources on defensive measures?

In this respect, there have been numerous studies concerning the impact of defensive medicine on skyrocketing healthcare costs. The survey results are remarkably consistent and reliable, with the vast majority of physician-respondents identifying the practice as an integral part of their daily routine. It's all about needless spending in order to avoid getting sued. Estimates of what purely defensive tests and procedures cost vary, but two recent studies pegged the percentages at 26 and 34 percent of total costs, respectively.[34]

Think about it: this *one* factor contributes so much to health cost inflation and yet the most significant overhaul since the advent of Medicare and Medicaid didn't address it. In fact, despite repeated Republican attempts to amend liability protections into the bill, the entire Obamacare debate unfolded with this important issue but a sideshow to the President's relentless rhetorical campaign against greedy insurance carriers and bottom-line focused employers.

Anyone mildly interested in politics understands the influence trial lawyers have within the Democratic Party. This specialty bar and its political action committees give 98 percent of their political campaign dollars to Democrats.[35]

This relatively small group exerts monumental influence over the Party, its candidates, and the national platform. I should know; nowhere does this powerful interest group have more influence than in deep blue Maryland, where trial bar legislators control every committee with jurisdiction over state tort law.

My experience as a pro tort reform governor provides insight into why a popular president would forego antagonizing the national trial bar, and why most states have such difficulty in passing reforms that limit medical malpractice premium increases.[36]

Similar to other states, Maryland physicians in 2003-2004 were hit with huge malpractice rate hikes that led to any number of bad impacts for Maryland's citizens, from doctor shortages in the rural areas of the state to premature retirements by well known older specialists. In effect, so many physicians were simply unwilling or unable to pay outrageous premium increases in order to maintain their practice. My attempt to push through watered down liability reforms during a special session of the legislature was not only rebuffed, but it led to a doubling down of bad policy as trial lawyer members and their allies replaced legal reforms with a new tax on health maintenance organizations.

One searing memory from that chapter occurred as I entered the historic Maryland State House on the day of the vote. I was greeted by the sight of well-known plaintiff attorneys from around the country buttonholing members as they gathered outside the House and Senate chambers. Instantly, I knew we were cooked. There was no way back-bench Democrats otherwise interested in passing a meaningful bill were going to turn on the group that fed them. And so it came to pass, as my veto of a reform-absent tax increase on HMOs was overridden, with just three House Republicans voting with the majority Democrats.

Come to think about it, it was predictable that the morphing of a malpractice reform bill into a tax increase vehicle would replicate itself during the Obamacare debate. One obvious takeaway: progressives and their liberal allies will always seek to change the target from medical malpractice reform to big, bad business interests. This tactic fits well with an anti-corporate mentality and the familiar class warfare rhetorical onslaught perfected by the contemporary left.

The political lessons here are straightforward. Despite public opinion to the contrary, it is never easy to pass meaningful liability relief where trial lawyer influence is strong. The accompanying economic calculus is equally easy to follow: serious malpractice reforms tend to lower medical malpractice awards, which tend to lower the contingency fees earned by trial lawyers, which tend to diminish the size and scope of political contributions to plaintiff-friendly legislators, the vast majority of whom are Democrats.

Digging Out: Fix Medicare

Obamacare suffers from another major policy omission: lack of entitlement reform. Specifically, the bill's failure to address the single largest contributor to our long-term budget deficit: Medicare. This circa 1965 giant healthcare program for the elderly suffers from uncontrollable costs and a failure of political will to do something about it. Now close to 50 years old, it remains a defined benefit plan immunized from cost reforms in light of its immense popularity with senior citizens. The reader may be familiar with the popular bumper sticker: "I'm a senior citizen and I vote." The not-so-subtle message: do not under any circumstances mess with my Medicare benefits. Accordingly, most recent GOP attempts to slow the growth of Medicare spending have been met with successful "Medi-scare" campaigns directed at the over 65 crowd. For recent context, one need look no further than "New York 26," the special election held in New York's 26th Congressional District in May of 2011.

In that race, liberal Democrat Kathy Hochul claimed an upset victory over Republican Assemblywoman Jane L. Corwin in a historically GOP leaning district. The win set off familiar shockwaves throughout American politics. Familiar because a heavily-financed "Medi-scare" strategy had again achieved a predictable result. Yet again, Congressional Democrats had succeeded at demonizing a GOP attempt to reform a Medicare program rapidly heading toward bankruptcy. Equally predictable, a Republican majority had again failed to make the case for necessary reforms, which in this case was a Congressman Paul Ryan-forged proposal to provide Medicare choice through a private voucher system. In retrospect, an upset here was not so surprising; a voting population older than the national average and poor economy made for fertile demagogic ground.

Politics is a front-running business, so it took no time for some GOP Monday morning quarterbacks to question the Ryan budget strategy. The complaints were familiar: Why lead with our chin? Why did we feel compelled to propose a Medicare reform when the President had never bothered to do so? Can't we come up with a strategy to counter those ruthlessly effective scare ads?

I experienced a similar attack during my Congressional tenure, when a confident Speaker Newt Gingrich predicted that a series of market reforms would over time leave traditional Medicare to "whither on the vine." In baseball parlance, it was a high fastball right down the middle of the plate. Immediately, an energized

Democratic minority transformed the prediction into political gold. Finally, the Republicans had come clean. The progressives' worst fears were confirmed. The GOP aimed to end Medicare as we know it. Their Speaker said so. All of which led to millions of negative ads targeted to seniors.

Despite a safe seat, I too spent many hours at constituent gatherings explaining what the Speaker *really* meant to say. Not such a big deal for a safe Member, but a monumental deal for those in marginal seats or with large senior communities. The old adage, "when you're explaining, you're losing," applies here. Marginal seat members never appreciate being forced on the defensive given the margins that define their districts. And attempting to explain complicated changes to a popular entitlement such as Medicare only makes matters worse.

One (further) unfortunate point regarding Medicare politics: the political identity of a proposed reform *counts*. "New York 26" again proved the effectiveness of generational warfare tactics. Yet, Obamacare reduces Medicare spending by $700 billion over ten years, with most of the cuts targeted to hospitals, skilled nursing facilities, and hospices. Some may recall the Romney campaign's attempt to make this an issue during the summer of 2012. But the political fallout was zero. Indeed, although many seniors opposed Obamacare, the reliably Democratic leaning A.A.R.P. openly supported it, thereby minimizing Romney's attempted counter-offensive on the Democratic Party's most prized issue. Here, the party provided the required cover for what could have been political Armageddon.

The odds of generating a serious national debate about spending and entitlement reform are always long. Federal budget calculations are mind numbing. The policy options are distasteful. And then there are those shameless attack ads so easily brought to television screens across America. After all, it's so much easier to demonize Paul Ryan than grasp concepts such as discretionary spending caps, mandatory outlays, and interest payments on the national debt.

One of the great, unanalyzed lessons of politics is that it is always easier to do *nothing*, as opposed to *something*. The voters tend to have stronger attitudes about *something*, especially when *something* brings about real change. And most especially when that change impacts a sacrosanct entitlement such as Medicare. On the other side is *nothing*. *Nothing* means kicking the proverbial can down the road until the next election. Pundits might complain about *nothing* and it certainly polls poorly. But they don't get up in arms about it. After all, there is *nothing* to get excited about.

Should *something* ever become a realistic goal, it would require liberals and conservatives to negotiate *real* savings within Medicare's existing structure.

On the right, there is likely enough GOP support for additional means testing of benefits (requiring additional dollars from those who can most afford it), increasing the Medicare eligibility age from 65 to 67 (reflecting an adjustment to today's longer life spans), and extending lower prescription drug rebates by requiring drug companies to pay higher Medicare rebates for older, dual-eligible senior citizens. Indeed, Republicans are already on record in favor of the Ryan voucher proposal. These reforms are not without political pain, but past budget negotiations have produced considerable conservative, and some Democratic support for all of them.

Any attempt to pry real savings from the left will be more difficult. State reapportionment has generated more safe seats and more ideological members on both sides of the aisle. For Congressional Democrats, that means additional votes dedicated to growing and protecting federal entitlements, generally without regard to the fiscal health of the program. And, more importantly, it means no shifting of costs on to the backs of existing beneficiaries. Accordingly, the potentially greatest cost saving measures (increasing the Part B premium or limiting cost sharing under Medigap policies) would be highly problematic for today's Democratic Members.

A series of baseline questions present themselves: Can a sense of immediacy be generated about a topic as dry as the federal budget? Is the American middle class willing to give up favored preferences in the name of fiscal sanity? Will Democrats *ever* agree to serious entitlement reforms?

Difficult questions lead to a simple answer: Congress will act the first time a serious reform proposal, such as the Ryan plan, is not punished at the polls. In effect, it's up to the people to grasp the depth of the problem and reward those willing and able to do something about it. Unfortunately, our political culture's track record here is not so promising. One can *hope* (to borrow a phrase), however.

Digging Out: The Medicaid Challenge

As a former governor, I am acutely aware of Medicaid's fiscal upside and downside. The popular federal-state program pays states between 50-83 cents on each dollar spent on medical care for the poor and working poor. Poorer states receive formulaic higher matches. In this respect, the program represents an essential element of a (state based) social safety net. Coverage of certain base populations is mandatory, although states may at their discretion choose to cover additional populations and provide additional medical services. And herein lies the rub, as the states have gradually expanded Medicaid coverage during good times and bad.

Unfortunately, Obamacare expands Medicaid's partnership with the states to unprecedented levels by covering individuals up to 133 percent (really 138 percent since five percent of an individual's income is disregarded) of the federal poverty line.[37] The prize in this Cracker Jacks box? The federal government will cover all of the costs generated by new enrollees for three years. Note that the "bargain" does not cover the bills for Medicaid-eligible individuals who had previously failed to sign up for the program. States will have to pick them up at their existing match rate.[38]

Nevertheless, some may conclude the states come out the big winner, as more of their citizens get covered and the feds pay the entire tab for the initial thirty-six months. No such luck, however.

At the state level, Medicaid has been spiraling out of control for years. Presently, it eats up 24% percent of state budgets and shows no sign of slowing down.[39] So, Obamacare's mandate that states pick up those who were previously eligible but had failed to sign up will only exacerbate their budget dilemmas. Further, the 100 percent match ends at three years; states will be required to pick up *some* percentage of the match after that date. Again, more entitlement expansion and more mandatory spending for cash-strapped states.

The Supreme Court's Obamacare decision overturned one especially egregious piece of the bill: that states would be forced to participate in Medicaid expansion or face the loss of existing federal Medicaid funding. The majority opinion made clear that states which chose to forego compliance with Medicaid expansion can lose only *new* Medicaid funding from the feds, not all of their present Medicaid matching dollars. Such a draconian cut was viewed as an unconstitutional crossing of the line.[40] Accordingly, governors will think long and hard about the costs and benefits associated with their potential new pile of money—and related fiscal strings. A few have already declined the new money, while a number of legislatures have independently sought to prevent their governors from participation in the new coverage requirements.

Parenthetically, the old Washington line, "if *we* don't do it somebody else will get the money" (for once) does not apply. Obamacare makes clear that no other state will receive additional dollars in such an event. Leading researchers have concluded that the cost of Medicaid expansion could be cut by $424 billion (over the next eight years) if the 18 states that have previously opted out (as of April 30, 2013) do not change their minds.[41]

Sticker Shock

It does not take a budget guru to figure out the macro impact of Obamacare's Medicaid expansion: what was a rapidly spiraling out-of-control budget item will now be a wildly spiraling out-of-control budget item. Only this time the federal taxpayer will be on the hook. For those of you keeping score, that would be an additional $443.5 billion (from 2014 to 2019) on top of the previous $5 trillion in debt racked up during the Obama admin-istration's first four years in office.[42]

Obamacare's respective authors most assuredly foresaw the eighteen million (and counting) new Medicaid enrollees. It is un-fortunately prototypical of the left to play "kick the can" with federal expenditures that will not lead to catastrophic crises until they are out of office. In fact, a program originally meant to serve poor women with children will now cover in excess of 80,000,000 Americans. That means approximately a quarter of the US population would fall under Uncle Sam's healthcare hand.[43] A program so large and entrenched would be nearly impossible to reform; yet another appealing aspect of Obamacare for all those social engineers situated within the Obama White House.

Digging Out: Stop the Job-Bleeding

A final component to the real life consequences of Obamacare's employer mandate (requiring employers with 50 or more employees to provide coverage) is the impossible-to-escape conclusion that higher costs per employee translate into fewer employees. For qualifying employers, per-employee costs will rise at least $2,000; employers that continue to offer health insurance will see still higher costs. It's all private sector *Economics 101*, wherein businesses with mandated higher labor costs will simply seek to reduce the cost of labor. American businesses appear ready to buy into this general rule of economics. A recent US Chamber of Commerce survey revealed that 74 percent of small businesses believe Obamacare will make it more difficult to hire new employees.[44] Even more damning is the Congressional Budget Office's estimate that the regulatory and tax burdens brought about by the new healthcare mandates will lead to 800,000 fewer workers by the end of 2020.[45]

Another aspect of Obamacare's desultory impact on employment is the perverse incentive to hire part-time rather than full-time workers.

As we've seen, Obamacare's mandatory employer penalty provision kicks in at 50 employees. The penalty is calculated by the total number of full-time equivalent employees, minus 30 full-time employees. Part-time workers are not part of the penal equation. Hence, the law creates incentive to hire part-time rather than full-time employees.

Two examples:

COMPANY A: 45 full-time employees
+10 part-time employees

---

50 full-time equivalent employees

COMPANY A's penalty for failure to offer health insurance is as follows:
45 full-time employees
-30 full-time employees (statutory formula)

---

15 x $2,000 = $30,000

COMPANY B has: 40 full-time employees
+20 part-time employees

---

50 full-time equivalent employees

COMPANY B's penalty for failure to offer health insurance is as follows:
40 full-time employees
-30 full-time employees (statutory formula)

---

10 x $2,000 = $20,000

As the President is fond of saying, "do the math." But this math does not work. You see, successful employers are generally rational actors; they seek to maximize profit and minimize costs. As applied to Obamacare, many smaller employers will seek to stay under the 50-employee threshold by curtailing their hiring or converting full-time employees to part-time status. As stated, numerous well known retailers and restaurant chains (Red Lobster, Kroger, Darden) have announced employee cuts in advance of full Obamacare implementation in 2014.[46] Is there any wonder why part-time job growth accounted for three out of every four new jobs created during the year immediately prior to full scale implementation?[47]

Obamacare requires a massive transfer of dollars from the private to the public sector. These dollars will fund a gigantic new federal entitlement that impacts 16 percent of the US economy. Dollars that were originally targeted to investment opportunities, (those that produce jobs and profits), will now be redirected to government. The result is a dramatic assault on job creation: Obamacare's regulatory compliance costs and tax increases make it more expensive to invest *and* hire full time workers in the real world. A restaurant chain CEO stated as much in Obamacare-related testimony before the US House of Representatives Committee on Oversight and Government Reform in July of 2011:

> It is important to note that the PPACA explicitly makes labor more expensive. It is completely predictable that businesses such as ours will search for ways to take jobs out of our existing restaurants to reduce that expense. . . . We would undoubtedly increase the number of part time employees; decrease the number of full time employees and attempt to automate positions (such as replacing cashier positions with ordering kiosks). These are not actions we would choose to take. They are actions the PPACA will all but compel us to take. . . . Under the PPACA, we would have little choice other than to reduce

[capital expenditures], eliminating jobs and endangering the long-term prospects of our business.

—ANDREW PUZDER,
CEO of CKE Restaurants Inc.[48]

The bottom line: less private sector revenue means less private sector profit, which means less private sector jobs, which means less private sector growth.

For the country, all this is yet another reminder about the progressive business cycle: more mandates mean additional costs, which translate into reduced job creation in the private sector.

A Missed Opportunity

I have given dozens of speeches around the country over the past three years. My topic is usually some aspect of American politics. Frequently, the talks are followed by a lengthy question and answer period. It should come as no surprise that just about every Q&A session includes one or more queries about Obamacare. My habit is to answer the question, but never hesitate to add that the President missed a real opportunity to pass comprehensive, bipartisan healthcare reform; that a Republican House majority would have supported a package of more modest reforms targeted to affordability and cost-containment; that allowing health insurance policies to be written across state lines is a workable idea; that community health centers located in poor communities do a good job of serving the needs of the poor and working poor; that encouraging state-based legal reform measures would mitigate the impact of defensive medicine; that properly constructed high risk insurance pools are more cost effective than elimination of pre-existing condition disclaimers; that Health Savings

Accounts are popular because they work; that there exists a Republican willingness to increase the Medicare eligibility age and means test benefits for wealthier seniors; that banning lifetime benefit limits, capping out-of-pocket expenses, and imposing mandatory lower deductibles are sure to drive health insurance premiums higher in the individual and group markets; and that a super progressive President and Congressional leadership were far more interested in social engineering our healthcare delivery system than securing meaningful cost control. An almost 1,000 page bureaucratic monster with countless additional mandates, onerous new taxes, and 16,000 additional IRS agents was the unfortunate result.

It Lives

From a political perspective, a single-payer inspired President was determined to expand federal control over our healthcare delivery system. Almost four years of a president's political capital was expended on healthcare at a time America was experiencing a lackluster, jobless recovery. Unemployment in excess of seven percent since the beginning of the Obama administration speaks to the underlying public malaise and private sector uncertainty of the era.

It bears repeating that the Obama administration hatched a sweeping program of government control over 16 percent of the American economy in the face of strenuous opposition from the same job creators government typically looks to in order to grow out of recessions. And it is the primary job generators (small businesses with 50 or more employees) who will now be forced to purchase health insurance or pay a fine. A predictable reaction: small businesses will shed workers to save labor costs, increase automation to save labor costs, and/or cut their full time payroll to save labor costs. An equally predictable result: some previously uninsured workers become covered, and some previously employed workers become unemployed. Not a helpful result for America's marginal workforce.

At the other end of the spectrum is what Obamacare fails to do, most importantly its inability to control rapidly escalating healthcare costs. With the exception of newly formed state insurance exchanges and a scheduled large cut in Medicare reimbursements (which nobody believes will actually take place), most of Obamacare's policy provisions have little to do with structural cost controls. Indeed, Obamacare represents an enormously enlarged government footprint that will make our healthcare delivery system ever more expensive. The absence of any meaningful legal reform is the most obvious missing element here, and also the most under-reported.

What Could Have Been

In the end, Obamacare means we spend more dollars, generate more debt, invent more government, lose more jobs, manufacture more complexity, cause more uncertainty, *and* fail to deliver desperately needed entitlement reform. The American public recognizes a bad law when it sees one. And the Administration does too. Check it out: no fewer than four provisions of the original statute (Medicare cuts, the employer mandate, eligibility requirements for insurance subsidies, and caps on out-of-pocket costs) were given delayed effective dates due to a federal bureaucracy ill prepared for a monstrous blizzard of new rules and a private sector ill equipped to harmonize separate and independent computer systems.

Pundits point out that this initial wave of Administration-sponsored delays seems timed to get negative Obamacare reviews off the front page until after the mid-term elections of November, 2014. This may be true, but any delay in Obamacare implementation should be a welcome development. Indeed, it is the commonsense majority's task to delay, oppose, challenge, or starve the remaining draconian provisions of the statute before full implementation in 2014 and thereafter.

Or, the voters could simply elect a veto-proof Republican Congress in order to further delay (some of) the bad law's effective dates. Sort of like a regulatory purgatory, but without a lot of new taxes. All goals worth contemplating as the punishing consequences of Obamacare hit home with an increasingly anxious public.

Selling Obamacare

I could not conclude this chapter without at least a passing citation to the great ironies within the context of Obamacare's post-passage marketing plan.

The Obama White House has rather famously undertaken an "educational" blitz in order to more effectively sell its new product to a skeptical public. Academics, actors, and athletes were approached to help market a law whose approval had fallen to the mid-30s by the summer of 2013.[49]

On the grassroots front, the Obama campaign army was called out of retirement. The mission was familiar: get the young people excited—just as they did the last two presidential election cycles.

But the third attempt proved to be a bridge too far. Seems a lot of the heretofore youthful enthusiasts had been bitten by the long arm of Obamacare premium increases.[50] Young, healthy college stuents found themselves in the immediate crosshairs, as heretofore low premium, defined cap plans offered by colleges and universities felt Obamacare's inflationary impact.[51]

At Lenoir-Rhyne University in North Carolina, administrators saw a premium increase from $245.00 per student in 2012 to $2,500.00 per student in 2013.[52] Similarly, premiums at the University of Puget Sound increased from $165 to between $1,500 and $2,000 over the same one year period.[53] Not surprisingly, other schools simply dropped student coverage due to the high cost.[54]

Similar inflation hit the individual market, as healthy, single adults were forced to choose between premium increases of 40% or more or pay a fine to the federal government. Alas, many of the heretofore youthful enthusiasts figured out they could save money by simply paying the mandate penalty for failing to secure insurance.[55]

The President's youth-focused pitch touted Obamacare's much ballyhooed consumer protections (premium tax credits for young adults, elimination of pre-existing condition disclaimers, extended coverage on parents' health insurance until age 26, no co-pays for mammograms, birth control, and sexual and domestic violence screenings). But many young Americans remained unimpressed—assurances from Bon Jovi and Oprah notwithstanding.

| HEALTHCARE SECURITY CHAPTER FOOTNOTES |

1. "Harry Reid: Obamacare Train Wreck Needs More Money," *Independent Journal Review*, May 7, 2013.
2. Sean A. Timmons, "Fraud and Abuse Provisions in the Patient Protection and Affordable Care Act as Amended by the Health Care and Education Reconciliation Act," www.smithlaw.comhttp://www.smithlaw.com/publications/Fraud%20and%20Abuse%20Article%20from%20May%202010%20Prognosis.pdf
3. Americans for Limited Government Research Foundation, *ObamacareReg Watcher*, Volume 2, Issue 5, May 2011.
4. Ibid.
5. Ibid.
6. Robert Pear, "Compromise Idea for the Insuring of Birth Control," *The New York Times*, February 2, 2013.
7. Michael Scherer, "Rick Santorum Wants to Fight 'The Dangers of Contraception,'" swampland.time.com, February 14, 2012.
8. "Notre Dame sues Obama Administration over HHS rule," *The Washington Examiner*, http://washingtonexaminer.com/article/1304566#.UKv9zuRQRIE
9. Shawn Tully, "Documents reveal AT&T, Verizon and others, thought about dropping employer-sponsored benefits," *Fortune*, May 6, 2010.
10. The survey found that 50% of employers would "definitely" or "probably" examine alternatives to their current coverage once Obamacare is fully implemented.
11. Ibid: the estimate was provided by McKinsey analyst Alissa Meade to a group of health insurance executives in November 2010.
12. CBO and JCT Report : H.R. 4872 The Reconciliation Act of 2010, March 20, 2010.
13. "By delaying Obamacare's employee mandate, did the White House also delay the individual mandate?" *Forbes*, July 8, 2013.
14. Larry Clifton, "Obamacare at Play in 2012 Election," *Digital Journal*, September 28, 2011.

15. Ibid.

16. Ibid.

17. Janet Adamy and Melanie Trottman, "Some Unions Grow Wary of Health Law They Backed," *The Wall Street Journal*, January 31, 2013, pg. A1.

18. John Fund, "Putting Lipstick on the Obamacare Pig," National Review Online, April 21, 2013.

19. http://blogs.wsj.com/corporate-intelligence/2013/07/12/union-letter-obamacare-will-destroy-the-very-health-and-wellbeing-of-workers/

20. "IRS Employees Union is 'very concerned' about being required to enroll in Obamacare's health insurance exchanges," *Forbes*, July 26, 2013.

21. Howard Dean, "The Affordable Care Act's rate-setting won't work," *The Wall Street Journal*, July 28, 2013.

22. Ibid; see also HR 452 introduced by Representative Phil Roe (R-Tenn.) which would terminate IPAB.

23. Ibid.

24. Ibid.

25. In *Gonzales v. Raigh*, Scalia sided with the court's liberal minority in holding that the cultivation and consumption of marijuana for medical purposes qualified as "commerce . . . .within the several states." See: Damon Root, "Antonin Scalia's Obamacare Problem," *Reason Magazine*, March 1, 2012.

26. Chief Justice John Roberts Opinion, *National Federation of Independent Business et al. v. Sebelius, Secretary of Health and Human Services, et al.*, October 2011, http://www.supremecourt.gov/opinions/11pdf/11-393c3a2.pdf

27. Andrew Lundeen, "Obamacare tax increase will impact us all," The Tax Foundation: TaxFoundation.org, March 5, 2013.

28. Ibid.

29. Sally Snipes, "In 2013, Millions Of Americans Face Obamacare Tax Hikes," *Forbes*, December 25, 2012.

30. Sam Baker, "Device-makers say tax will cost 43,000 US jobs," *The Hill, September 7, 2011.*

31. Gregory Sorenson, "The White House Brain Initiative Hits a Tax Hurdle," *The Wall Street Journal*, April 15, 2013.

32. Curtis Dubay, "Tax increases in the Patient Protection and Affordable Care Act," *The Heritage Foundation,* January 20, 2011. http://www.heritage.org/research/reports/2011/01/obamacare -and-new-taxes-destroying-jobs-and-the-economy

33. Michael Miller, "Harry Reid: Obamacare Train Wreck Needs More Money," *Independent Journal Review,* May 7, 2013.

34. "Physician Study: Quantifying the Cost of Defensive Medicine: Lawsuit driven medicine creates $650-850 billion in annual healthcare costs," Jackson Healthcare, http://www.jacksonhealth-care.com/healthcare-research/healthcare-costs-defensive-medicine-study.aspx

35. Center for Responsive Politics: American Association for Justice Summary, http://www.opensecrets.org/pacs/lookup2.php?strID= C00024521&cycle=2010

36. A cautionary note for all aggressive tort reformers. My battle with the Trial Bar was waged in the appropriate venue: the state legislature. Although some on the right disagree, there is a solid case to be made that Tenth Amendment considerations dictate that tort reform debates play out at the state level. But one may possess real doubts such Constitutional considerations played a part in the Obama administration's decision to take a pass on liability reforms within Obamacare. As stated, plaintiffs' attorneys and their political action committees give more than 90% of their political contributions to Democrats; hence, the lack of meaningful tort reform measures within the Affordable Care Act.

37. Michael S. Greve, "The states will lose on Medicaid," *National Review Online,* January 12, 2012. http://www.nationalreview.com/ articles/287926/states-will-lose-medicaid-michael-s-greve

38. Ibid.

39. Ibid.

40. Robert Samuelson, "The Medicaid Albatross," *Real Clear Politics,* July 23, 2012. http://www.realclearpolitics.com/arti-cles/2012/07/23/the_medicaid_albatross_114865.html

41. Kaiser Family Foundation, Goldwater Institute, cited in: Christina Corieri, "States can save taxpayers $609 billion," *The Wall Street Journal,* May 1, 2013.

42. Sarah Kliff, "The Supreme Court forces states to make a big Medicaid decision. Here's how they'll do it," *The Washington Post,* June 29, 2012. Estimate by John Holahan of the Urban Institute.

43. Pam Bondi (Attorney General of Florida), " Feds Power Grab Must Be Stopped," *Politico,* March 12, 2012. http://www.politico.com/news/stories/0312/73853.html

44. United States Chamber of Commerce, "United States Chamber of Commerce Q4 Small Business Study," available at http://www.uschambersmallbusinessnation.com/uploads/Chamber%20Q4_Summary%20Memo_Final%20.pdf.

45. J. Lester Feder and Kate Nocera, "CBO: Health law to shrink workforce by 800,000," POLITICO PRO, February 10, 2011, available at http://www.politico.com/news/stories/0211/49273.html.

46. "Prepping for Obamacare, Chain Cut Workers' Hours," The Associated Press, October 9, 2012.

47. www.reuters.com, "Analysis: Obamacare, tepid U.S. growth fuel part-time hiring, August 21, 2013.

48. Andrew Puzder (CEO of CKE Restaurants Inc.), Hearing Testimony for "Impact of Obamacare on Job creators and their decision to offer health insurance," Committee on Oversight and Government Reform: Subcommittee on Health Care, District of Columbia, Census and National Archives, July 28, 2011, p. 22.

49. An August, 2013 Wall Street Journal/NBC News poll had 47% opposed to the healthcare overhaul and only 34% in support. Political independents opposed the bill by a 30% margin; see also, medicaldaily.com, "Spurned by NFL, Obama enlists Hollywood to market "Obamacare," July 23, 2013.

50. The same poll found only 37% of young adults thought the law a good idea.

51. Avik Roy, "Yet another White House Obamacare delay: out-of-pocket caps waived until 2015", www.forbes.com, August 8, 2013.

52. Ibid.

53. Ibid.

54. Ibid.

55. The National Center for Public Policy Research concluded that nearly 4 million single, childless people between the ages of 18 and

34 would save $500.00 if they declined Obamacare insurance options next year. This figure includes projected Obamacare subsidies for their insurance premiums. The Center also estimated that over 3 million would save $1,000 or more. See Press Release, The National Center for Public Policy Research, August 15, 2013.

NOT SO SECURE
SOCIAL SECURITY

"We shall make the most lasting progress if we recognize that social security can furnish only a base upon which each one of our citizens may build his individual security through his own individual efforts."

—FRANKLIN D. ROOSEVELT

I t's the granddaddy of federal programs. Nine out of ten Americans age 65 and older receive its benefits. It's the most sacrosanct entitlement. Its political appeal is off the charts. It's the true third rail of American politics. But it's in real trouble, and few politicians of either party appear ready, willing, or able to do what needs to get done in order to ensure its long term health or even to discuss it as a problem that needs to be solved. As a consequence of avoiding the issue, many—and per-haps most—recipients misperceive that they are receiving only what they contributed plus interest. In reality, for most folks it amounts to much, much more.

Earlier I detailed how even marginal attempts to bring change to Medicare were fraught with political peril. Chapter and verse with regard to the "Mediscare" tactics employed in New York's 26th Congressional district in 2011 serve to remind all of us about the difficulties associated with any proposal intended to limit or reform a popular federal entitlement.

It is a widely held view that any such attempt brought to Social Security will face a similar fate. And this is despite the by-now increasingly dire warnings from the Trustees charged with maintaining the Trust Funds' fiscal integrity. Recent experience under Bush era proposals makes the point. Those who dare challenge the status quo will face serious political consequences. But before we further explore the many obstacles in the way of any present day rescue, it makes sense to re-familiarize ourselves with Social Security's origins and evolution over its 78-year existence.

History of Social Security

The Social Security Administration's website traces the history of the program to the years after the Civil War.[1] Casualties on both sides were enormous; the toll left hundreds of thousands of widows, orphans, and disabled servicemen. This large and largely unemployable population required considerable government assistance and led to the creation of a federally sponsored pension program for soldiers. Yet, no non-military safety net for retired Americans would come about for another 60 years. [2]

Civics textbooks credit the industrial revolution with the rapid development of American cities during the first decades of the 20th century. The promise of better wages and a higher standard of living generated a major migration from the farm. A more efficient sanitation and health infrastructure followed suit, contributing to a dramatic increase in average lifespan. Indeed, the first three decades of the century marked the fastest increase in longevity in human history, as the number of senior citizens reached 7.8 million by 1935.[3] A larger, older populace generated demands for greater economic security. The calls were answered when Congress passed and President Roosevelt signed The Social

Security Act in August of 1935. The concept of a guaranteed retirement income was now firmly vested in the American psyche. A real social safety net for older Americans was now the law of the land. Older Americans would be direct beneficiaries of this new social welfare program. But American politics would never be the same.

Social Security's rather humble beginnings pale in comparison to the gigantic federal entitlement it is today. Growth has been rapid and clearly unsustainable. Consider the trajectory of benefits paid over the past seventy-three years:

Total benefits paid 1940: $35 million

1950: $961 million

1960: $11.2 billion

1970: $31.9 billion

1980: $120.5 billion

1990: $247.8 billion

2009: $685.8 billion

2012: $760 billion[4]

Total benefits paid for 2009 appear here for a reason: this was the last year Social Security collected more in taxes than it paid out in benefits. As such, 2010 marked the beginning of a cash flow deficit that Social Security's trustees and the Congressional Budget Office believe will last for the next 75 years, and probably never end.[5] In fact, the latest estimates have the annual deficit growing every year for the next 18 years, when it will level off at approximately $350 billion dollars a year (in 2010 numbers)[6]. But what of the present assets within the Social Security Trust Fund? Where is the cash surplus that built up over the years?

The "Lock Box"

One of the enduring Saturday Night Live skits of recent vintage was the mock debates between Will Ferrell (playing Governor George W. Bush) and Darrell Hammond (playing Vice President Al Gore). The skits were quite funny and the partisan hits were pretty evenly matched. But it was Hammond's repeated use of the phrase "lock box" that produced guaranteed laughter. The phrase referred to the Vice President's circa 2000 campaign pledge to begin segregating Social Security contributions into what he called a "lock box"—a place where contributions would be safe from the federal government's insatiable appetite to spend.

Many Americans focused on the drawn out, comical enunciation of the phrase rather than the point at issue. To wit, the $2.5 trillion in surplus contributions that Social Security collected between 1983 and 2009. But the money that was supposed to be set aside in the trust fund ("lock box") was spent. The federal government had gone on a bipartisan spending binge; the dollars intended for Al Gore's lock box were treated just like every other federal dollar received and spent by the federal government. Quite literally there was no physical setting aside of any money exclusively for Social Security.

Today, special issue Treasury bonds are the only assets in the Trust Fund. The Treasury must issue these bonds when Social Security runs a deficit. The bonds are not backed by any assets. They are simply a federal demand note on future revenues.[7]

The bottom line: one agency of the federal government (Treasury) promises to pay another federal entity (Social Security) the money the federal government has taken out and spent over the years. Accordingly, when the cash flow deficit hit in 2010, the Treasury began to redeem the bonds by using other federal funds to pay off the Social Security liens. This classic Ponzi scheme presents two big problems: (1.) The money to pay off the liens must come from more deficit spending; and (2.) the special issue bonds will run out around 2037. At that time, and pursuant to federal law, every retiree will suffer a benefits cut of about 22%. This almost impossible-to-comprehend result represents one of the few leverage points held by true reformers.

Advantages (and Disadvantages) of Longevity

How we dug this hole is not so difficult to understand—it's all in the numbers—and medical technology. As we have seen, life expectancy in the United States continues to expand: the lifespan of a 65-year-old in 1940 was 14 years; today it is almost 20 years.[8] The number of older Americans will double over the next 25 years.[9] In the real world, this means far fewer workers' contributions will support increasing numbers of retirees. For example, there were 42 workers for each Social Security beneficiary when the program began.[10] By 2001 the ratio was down to 3:4 workers per beneficiary.[11] Today that ratio has decreased to 2:1.[12] Advances in medical technology will most assuredly continue to lengthen American life spans. And this increased longevity will just as certainly make this ratio more problematic over time. So what is a wonderful result for the average citizen is not so good for the viability of the Social Security Trust Fund.

• • •

The Hard Way

The unsustainability of the present system is known to any and all who care to look. But what to do? Recent experience from the George W. Bush years reflects what *not* to do—at least if one expects to make any real progress toward entitlement reform.

It was not so long ago that a reasonably popular president decided to spend a portion of that popularity on a quite difficult task: push legislation to allow individuals to exercise a degree of control over their Social Security dollars. In other words, break the federal government's complete control over the use of an individual's mandatory Social Security contribution.

Such an initiative was not surprising to veteran Bush watchers. As far back as 2000, then-Governor Bush had advocated for personal retirement accounts as an adjunct to Social Security:

> Reform should include personal retirement accounts for young people—an element of all the major bipartisan plans. The idea works very simply. A young worker can take some portion of his or her payroll tax and put it in a fund that invests in stocks and bonds. We will establish basic standards of safety and soundness, so that investments are only in steady, reliable funds. There will be no fly-by-night speculators or day trading. And money in this account could only be used for retirement, or passed along as an inheritance.[13]

Five years later, President George W. Bush was ready to devote his reservoir of political good will to make a renewed pitch for private accounts. The setting was the President's State of the Union

Address. Republicans were in control of both Chambers. Social Security reform was a top domestic priority. And "W" unleashed a really big idea on the American public: "As we fix Social Security, we also have the responsibility to make the system a better deal for younger workers. And the best way to reach that goal is though voluntary personal retirement accounts."[14]

Reaction to the controversial proposal was hyper-partisan, and predictable. Among many familiar class warfare-induced responses came this from Rep. Louise M. Slaughter, D-NY: "President Bush wants to place the retirement needs of millions of hardworking women and families in the hands of his corporate cronies. Have we forgotten about Enron, WorldCom and Global Crossing? We cannot let this happen."[15]

And this from that old reliable class warrior, Senate Minority Leader Harry Reid: "There's a lot we can do to improve Americans' retirement security, but it's wrong to replace the guaranteed benefit that Americans have earned with a guaranteed benefit cut of 40% or more. Make no mistake, that's exactly what President Bush is proposing."[16]

Republican response was measured, but positive: "Tonight's speech set the stage for a vigorous debate on the future of Social Security. The president has proven he's a man of his word, and just as he pledged to add a prescription drug benefit to Medicare and delivered, I am confident he will spend the necessary amount of political capital to strengthen Social Security for today's seniors and future generations." —House Majority Whip Roy Blunt, R-MO.[17]

One senator highlighted the political courage behind the move: "I give the president credit for taking on a controversial issue (Social Security). Some elected officials want to ignore the problem except to make political hay out of it. But we're elected

to solve problems, not pass them on to the next generation."—
Sen. Charles Grassley, R-IA.[18]

Alas, lots of smoke (and thousands of miles on Air Force One)
produced no fire. A major public relations initiative directed by
the likes of presidential advisor Karl Rove and Republican National Committee Chairman Ken Mehlman failed to gain any
degree of traction. A nationwide grassroots tour to build public
support went nowhere. A significant decline in public opinion
polls for the President's handling of Social Security followed on
the heels of the less-than-successful series of tours.[19] And then
came the national trauma in the aftermath of Hurricane Katrina
and a quick end to what had been a promising beginning.

Pundits and Their Predictions

Political punditry, as engaged in by those who will never seek
elective office, is almost always a costless proposition; there is
no penalty attached to incorrect predictions, either optimistic
or dire. Rarely does the general public recall what is said by
most of the daily talking heads. Still, one of the more interesting aspects to literary research is to read past proclama-
tions by various pundits and then compare them to present
facts. One of my favorites in this regard is circa 2004 from the
well known liberal *New York Times* columnist Paul Krugman.
In a piece entitled "Inventing a Crisis," Krugman sought to
minimize Social Security's long-term woes while disparaging a
private account option:

> Right now the revenues from the payroll tax exceed the
> amount paid out in benefits. This is deliberate, the result

of a payroll tax increase—recommended by none other than Alan Greenspan—two decades ago. His justification at the time for raising a tax that falls mainly on lower- and middle-income families, even though Ronald Reagan had just cut the taxes that fall mainly on the very well-off, was that the extra revenue was needed to build up a trust fund. This could be drawn on to pay benefits once the baby boomers began to retire.

The grain of truth in claims of a Social Security crisis is that this tax increase wasn't quite big enough. Projections in a recent report by the Congressional Budget Office (which are probably more realistic than the very cautious projections of the Social Security Administration) say that the trust fund will run out in 2052. The system won't become "bankrupt" at that point; even after the trust fund is gone, Social Security revenues will cover 81 percent of the promised benefits. Still, there is a long-run financing problem.[20]

Note the citation to the year 2052 as the then-projected date for Social Security to run dry. The impossible to miss message: no problem here. 2052 is *so* many years away. Those doom-seeking Republicans are attempting to manufacture a phony crisis in order to make more money for their fat-cat friends on Wall Street. The message was in turn picked up by left-leaning interest groups such as moveon.org. This rabidly progressive group's spin on Social Security reform utilized an unpopular war to help make their case. It was a gift-wrapped "two-fer" for the George Soros-financed anti-war crowd. And they aimed to take maximum advantage of the moment. See for yourself the following text from a MoveOn.org print ad.

Now George Bush is misleading us about Social Security.

©2005 MoveOn.org

First George Bush said Saddam Hussein had weapons of mass destruction and a "mushroom cloud" was imminent. Now, he's claiming something equally outrageous; a phony Social Security "crisis."

George Bush claims Social Security will be "flat broke" and "bust" by the time today's workers retire. He says Social Security is going "bankrupt." Nothing could be further from the truth.

The facts are that Social Security can meet 100% of its obligations for the next 37 years with no changes to the current system, according to the Social Security Administration itself. Further, after 2042, the system reports it can pay more than 70% of benefits even if we do absolutely nothing. But we can, and should, do something.

People don't pay Social Security taxes on a penny of their income above $90,000 a year. Not a single penny. What if they did? The system would be in strong shape long after 2042.

But instead of the wealthy paying their fair share of Social Security taxes, George Bush is pushing the high-risk concept of Social Security privatization.

Privatization means cuts of up to 46% in guaranteed benefits, according to the Center for Budget and Policy Priorities.

Privatization means trillions of dollars in debt and billions in fees for George Bush's wealthy donors at financial institutions. And privatization means Social Security is no longer a guaranteed monthly check for

America's seniors, because the market can go down, not just up.

Social Security isn't "broke," "bankrupt," or in "crisis." And the sooner everyone—especially the media—begins to look at this administration's claims with a more skeptical eye, the better. So call your congressmen. Send in the coupon below and help us tell the truth about Social Security. And make sure you are not misled again.

This predictably leftist ad campaign suffered from one problem: by 2012, 2052 had become 2033, at least according to the Trustees that oversee Social Security's two trust funds. This more dire projection was dictated by elementary math: increased life spans, increased cost-of-living benefits, and a major wage dampening recession translate into more benefits and less revenue. Further pressure has been supplied by Obama-era efforts (from both parties) to lower the payroll tax (which helps fund Social Security) in order to stimulate employment.

The Clinton Era

It is a historical fact that three different Clinton era commissions offered Social Security reform plans that contained proposals for individual accounts. Another intriguing historical fact concerns Bill Clinton's personal interest in proposing private accounts.[21] Three former top advisors have stated as much.[22] The officials, including an assistant Treasury secretary (David Wilcox), a deputy assistant Treasury secretary (Douglas Elmendorf), and an aide to the National Economic Council (Jeffrey Liebman), told a Howard University conference in June of 2001 that the Clinton administration spent 18 months analyzing the viability of individual accounts.[23] Indeed, it appears that the President and his longtime antagonist, Speaker Newt Gingrich, had at some point reached a tentative deal to raise the retirement age and add a privately managed account option to a Social Security and Medicare reform package.[24] (Gingrich had advocated on behalf of such a plan for years.) The President was on board, but faced stiff resistance from the likes of Vice President Gore and Treasury Secretary Robert Rubin. Alas, even the best laid plans run into unforeseen obstacles. The sordid Monica Lewinsky affair and the accompanying specter of impeachment extinguished any such proposal. This unsightly chapter forced the self-proclaimed moderate to pivot left. It was now all (progressive) hands on deck; no further attention would be given to Social Security reform, period!

What To Do

Of the three major entitlement programs in serious need of reform, Social Security should be the least difficult to fix. Nevertheless, it will not be easy. Washington heavy lifting never is. And one of the primary rules of heavy lifting must be followed: some degree of bipartisan cooperation *must* accompany any major reform. On Capitol Hill, big things get accomplished only when some degree of bipartisan cooperation is found. Violations of this rule sentence whatever the "big thing" is to intense political sniping and negative polls. For recent context, just check out continuing public disapproval directed to the single party initiative called "Obamacare."

There are two ways to approach a solution to our Social Security crisis. One is to continue to advance the case that allowing workers to save and invest a portion of their contribution in a private account will create more wealth and relieve a portion of the fiscal pressure on the Trust Fund. The second is to acknowledge the political difficulties associated with changing the government's monopoly control over the system, and in turn work within Social Security's existing framework to effect change.

As described above, recent years have witnessed the tremendous political challenge associated with the creation of private accounts. The modern Democrat party appears fixated on the perpetuation of federal government control over what so many acknowledge is a broken system. Any serious proposal to empower individuals rather than government is guaranteed to create enormous opposition. And not only on Capitol Hill. Any proponent of private accounts will run headlong into a mainstream media onslaught. Every left-wing interest group in the country salivates at the opportunity to portray private account advocates as the tools of greedy Wall Street one percent-ers.

To be fair, few leaders in either party are willing to place their political careers in jeopardy in the face of such strong opposition. Without widespread societal recognition of a looming fiscal Armageddon, there is little reason to believe this reality will change anytime soon.

Accordingly, reformers are left with the more practical "Option B." Indeed, the recognition that "partial privatization" is off the table may lead some opponents into the "gotta get something done" mode. At least one can hope . . .

Generational Theft

Speaking of hope, younger workers must hope (and pray) that a courageous Congress and President will one day find the will to stop generational theft. Case-in-point: Social Security's actuaries project young people entering the workforce today stand to lose 4.2% of their total lifetime wages due to . . . Social Security.[25] The same economists say today's third graders will receive only 75 cents from each dollar (forcibly) contributed to the Fund over their lifetimes.[26] Contrast this inequity with (wealthier) workers nearing retirement age who can expect to collect a considerable profit.[27]

So what can and must get accomplished in the relatively short term? What component parts of the Trust Fund are most easily adjusted in order to secure solvency?

Practical Proposals

ELEMENT #1: BENEFITS

One way to ensure against millions of seniors sliding into retirement-induced poverty is to increase monthly Social Security payments in excess of the federal poverty line. On the other end of the income scale, means testing of wealthy seniors would place this population on a sliding scale to the point that the very affluent would be cut off from Social Security benefits. Surprisingly, perhaps, such a proposal has been advanced by the conservative Heritage Foundation.[28] This initiative could indeed achieve significant cost savings. The obvious disadvantage: it's not fair to penalize wealthy seniors simply because they are wealthy. But the foregoing is not a dominant concern of the upper class. Wealthy people do not rely on their monthly Social Security check. Most would not notice the minimal loss of income. The potential political appeal here is rather easy, too. The top 1% does not generate a lot of sympathy; neither should they generate enmity—but that's another story.

ELEMENT #2: RETIREMENT AGE

This is a no-brainer; the trend lines are clear as day. Americans will continue to live longer. In fact, many will live (and some will work) into their 70s and beyond. In the process, they will take out far more dollars than they contributed to the Trust Fund. Accordingly, it should not be a difficult task to (again) modestly raise the retirement age. It makes sense for a rational retirement age to be a function of life expectancy. Some further suggest indexing retirement to life expectancy going forward, an equitable way to achieve a rational relationship between the two.

A further sweetener for those who might wish to work beyond traditional retirement age: allow these workers to keep more after-tax income for as long as they do not claim benefits. The advantages of such a change are obvious: increased productivity from an extended work cycle and fewer recipients taking money out of the system. For those close to retirement age, however, present law should be maintained. It's only fair the federal government continue its moral responsibility to present day seniors. For everyone else, a change now will provide plenty of time to adjust one's individual retirement planning.

ELEMENT #3: ELIMINATE THE EARNINGS CAP

Many Americans do not realize that Social Security contributions of 6.2% are collected on the first $110,000 of earned income. This means Social Security is more regressive at the highest income levels than Medicare, wherein a 1.45% tax rate is applied to the full amount of earned income. It follows that removing Social Security's income cap would make the system more progressive. In this world, California Angels slugger

Albert Pujols would pay 1.45% on every one of his 25 million dollars a year, not simply the first $110,000. Conversely, a couple earning $220,000 or less would not pay a penny of additional tax.

The advent of means testing on the benefit side and the lifting of the $110,000 cap would make the system far more progressive. For those concerned about too much progressivity, a simple change is available: simply adjust the 6.2 percent downward. This trade-off would generate more enthusiasm on the right. In other words, wealthier Americans would enjoy a lower contribution rate in exchange for having lost their Social Security benefit cap at a specified income level.

ELEMENT #4: PRIVATE ACCOUNTS (KIND OF)

There may come a time in our politics when it will no longer be politically suicidal to support private accounts. Should this environment develop, the introduction of private accounts could more easily be accomplished *outside* of the existing system. One idea worth consideration: allow individuals to direct an *additional* contribution of 1, 2, or 3 percent into a private account on top of the present (6.2%) employee share under the payroll tax. The government could match this additional contribution, if it so chose.[29] The terms and conditions accompanying such an option could be modeled on the popular Roth IRA, wherein the account would be maintained for a certain number of years and withdrawals would be taken tax free. Any reasonable terms could be made a part of the private account, including limits on withdrawals. It bears repeating that this option would *not* be a part of traditional Social Security, but merely an additional investment option open to those who seek additional retirement income.

ELEMENT #5: CLEAN UP SSDI

Make no mistake. The Social Security disability program (SSDI) is in trouble. The SSDI Trust Fund could be exhausted by 2016, or possibly earlier.[30] And rather unsurprisingly, rapid expansion of the program appears to coincide with the tenure of the Obama administration. The numbers (and facts) as revealed in the Annual Social Security Trustees' report speak for themselves. A recent *Forbes* article pieced the ugly realities together quite cogently:

> Since our president entered the White House in January 2009 through September of this year 5.9 million people have been added to the SSDI or Social Security Disability program. That compares with less than 2.5 million jobs created during the same period. According to Social Security Administration data, currently including spouses and children, SSDI rolls have swollen to a bloated 10.9 million. A record one in fourteen workers is now on the SSDI dole. It's like checking in a hotel and never leaving. Of the 653,877 souls that departed the program in 2011, 36% departed by being gracious enough to die, while 52% reached retirement age and seamlessly switched to other benefits. Only 6% returned to work and 3.6% exited the program due to medical improvement. According to Congressional Research Services this program cost taxpayers $128.9 billion in 2011 and was in deficit to the tune of $25.3 billion. Funded by the 1.8% payroll tax and comprising nearly 18% of all social security spending, at current pace the trust fund may be exhausted by as early as 2015.[31]

Of course, the program has a legitimate purpose: to provide income assistance to individuals who are unable to find work as a result of a disability. It's all part of a social safety net most Americans support. But shared compassion has its limits. And one such line must be drawn at those who game the system in order to secure benefits.

How bad is the problem? So bad that the liberal Center for American Progress has opined the "program provides strong incentives to applicants and beneficiaries to remain permanently out of the labor force, and it provides no incentive to employers to implement cost-effective accommodations that enable employees with work limitations to remain on the job . . . too many work-capable individuals involuntarily exit the labor force and apply for, and often receive, "Social Security Disability Insurance."[32] Inappropriate awards also serve to discourage those who are legitimately in need of assistance. Today, some applicants wait as long as two years before their file is completed.[33] The old adage applies: justice delayed is justice denied.

But hope may be on the way. A 2012 Senate subcommittee's probe into the program revealed what an informed outside observer might have guessed: state and federal hearing examiners are often poorly trained, render inconsistent decisions, fail to follow required medical criteria, and use outdated occupational data to identify job openings for clients with partial disabilities.[34]

The same Congressional report presents a number of easily initiated, commonsense remedies, including the required attendance of the government's agency representative at evidentiary hearings, a stronger review process, an expanded (expert) consultative process, and an updated job and medical guideline vocational list.

SSDI has experienced excessive growth for a number of reasons. Large numbers of aging baby boomers certainly contribute to the growing numbers; more qualifiers simply translates into more applicants. But there is far more to the problem than simply numbers.

A portion of our problem is cultural. The "I'm getting mine" syndrome is a larger part of our nanny state culture than many of us care to admit. The Obama era certainly appears to feed the problem: 40% of the population was on one form or another of public assistance when the president took office. Today, that number stands at 55%.[35]

It's also the result of a generally lousy economy that compels those predisposed to public benefits to turn to the disability rolls.

Proposed remedies for what ails SSDI do not constitute heavy lifting. They can and should be adopted by a political class (allegedly) in the business of protecting and securing Social Security for future generations.

Going Forward

A cursory review of the literature reveals thousands of possible fixes to what ails Social Security. Accordingly, the foregoing suggestions are not meant to be exhaustive. But they do represent policy solutions that (1.) relieve the fiscal pressures on the Trust Funds, and (2.) appear to be politically viable. Not such a bad jumping off point for those interested in securing the future of this essential part of our social safety net.

.

| SOCIAL SECURITY CHAPTER FOOTNOTES |

1. Social Security Administration Website- History http://www.ssa.gov/
   history/briefhistory3.html
2. Ibid.
3. Ibid.
4. Ibid.
5. Stuart Butler, Alison Fraser, and Bill Beach, "Saving the American
   Dream: The Heritage Plan to fix the Debt, Cut Spending and Restore Prosperity," The Heritage Foundation, p.11 (2012).
6. Ibid.
7. Ibid.
8. Social Security Administration Website- Social Security Basic Facts
   http://www.ssa.gov/pressoffice/basicfact.htm
9. Ibid.
10. Ibid.
11. Ibid.
12. Ibid.
13. Quote taken from "The Final Report of the Presidents Commission
    to Strengthen Social Security," p.7. http://govinfo.library.unt.edu/
    csss/reports/Final_report.pdf (2002).
14. State of the Union Address (2008).
15. "Reaction to Bush's State of the Union Address," Associated Press
    from the USA Today Website, http://www.usatoday.com/news/
    washington/2005-02-02-quotes-reax-sou_x.htm
16. Ibid.
17. Ibid.
18. Ibid.
19. The Brookings Institution, "Why the 2005 Social Security Initiative
    Failed, and What it Means for the Future," September 21, 2007.
20. Paul Krugman, "Inventing a Crisis," (Op-Ed) The New York Times,
    December 7, 2004.
21. "Bill Clinton's Social Security Options," The Washington Post, Feb-
    ruary 29, 2005.

22. Michael D. Tanner, "Clinton Wanted Social Security Privatized," Cato Institute, July 13, 2001. http://www.cato.org/publications/commentary/clinton-wanted-social-security-privatized

23. Ibid.

24. Steven Gillon, *The Pact: Bill Clinton, Newt Gingrich and the Rivalry that Defined a Generation*, (Oxford University Press, 2008).

25. Geoffrey Canada, Stanley Druckenmiller, and Kevin Warsh, "Generational theft needs to be arrested," *The Wall Street Journal*, February 15, 2013.

26. Ibid.

27. Ibid.

28. Stuart Butler, Alison Fraser, and Bill Beach, "Saving the American Dream: The Heritage Plan to fix the Debt, Cut Spending and Restore Prosperity," The Heritage Foundation, p.11 (2012).

29. "The Final Report of the Presidents Commission to Strengthen Social Security," p.8 http://govinfo.library.unt.edu/csss/reports/Final_report.pdf

30. The 2012 Annual Report of the Board of Trustees of the Federal Old-Age and Survivors Insurance and Federal Disability Insurance Trust Funds.

31. Richard Finger, "Fraud and disability equal a multi billion dollar black hole for taxpayers," *Forbes*, January 14, 2013.

32. Center for American Progress, David H. Autor, Massachusetts Institute of Technology and NBER; Mark Duggan, University of Maryland and NBER, "Supporting work: a proposal for modernizing the U.S. disability insurance system," December, 2010.

33. United States Senate, Permanent Subcommittee on Investigations, Committee on Homeland Security and Governmental Affairs, "Social Security Disability programs: improving the quality of benefit award decisions," Minority Staff Report, September 13, 2012.

34. Ibid, Executive Summary, pp. 3-5.

35. Richard Finger, "Fraud and disability equal a multi billion dollar black hole for taxpayers," *Forbes*, January 14, 2013.

CONCLUSION

FDR famously promised Social Security would never become a way of life. John Kennedy assured the world that America would "pay any price" to expand freedom. Abraham Lincoln saw a united America as the "last best hope on earth." Ronald Reagan likened America to that "city on a hill"— a beacon of hope for an "afflicted mankind".

These unforgettable principles are presently being tested by the most tenacious of progressive administrations. Indeed, the terms and conditions of the American experience are now subject to daily inquisition by an empowered regulatory state taking dead aim at our economic assumptions and cultural aspirations. For this group, eighty years of steady government growth and the accompanying loss of individual freedom are not enough. A re-elected Obama is doubling down on federal healthcare, federal welfare, federal employment, federal student loans, and federal housing.

Yet, the societal ills described herein have grown in direct proportion to increasing federal intervention in our lives. And to make matters worse, this generation of progressive activists seeks to normalize such dysfunction on a regular basis.

Most Americans understand today's society is far more complex than that of Messrs. Washington, Jefferson, and Hamilton. They believe government has a role to play in the conduct of our daily lives. But they also see a gradual loss of individualism and corresponding growth of government dependence as detrimental to our national health and security. Importantly, many see the rising tide of government intervention as the major obstacle to the continuation of a generational sense of betterment that has made our experience so special, so unique.

But can this special combination of freedom and democracy be sustained? Human history would suggest "no." Indeed, the fundamentals of the human experience are distressingly familiar: government always grows; freedom always wanes. The lure of the nanny state has proven too tempting over the centuries. (Recall Margaret Thatcher's lament that "The only problem with socialism is that sooner or later you run out of other peoples' money.") Why then, would we expect our American experience to be different? Are we so exceptional to be immune from the tides of history?

My answer is no . . . and yes. We most certainly are not immune to historical trends; the gigantic size and seemingly endless reach of the federal government are plain for all to see. Obama-style progressivism has only made things worse. But we are still free. Belief in pluralism, federalism, and market capitalism remains strong in many parts of the country. And the notion of American exceptionalism has never lost its allure. Accordingly, all is not lost . . . if we are willing to stand up and say something.

This book is *my* turn to stand up and say something. My most sincere hope is that you too will feel compelled to stand up to all that is contributing to our national insecurity.

Over two hundred years ago, Edmund Burke cautioned that, "[t]he only thing necessary for the triumph [of evil] is for good men to do nothing." Please do not "do nothing." The fundamental values that define us are under extreme stress. But a national election, or two, can provide hope that things will change; that we will recapture the raw individualism and moral security we used to relish, even celebrate.

Won't you join in?

| ACKNOWLEDGMENTS |

There is one aspect of the literary world quite similar to politics: it's all about the team. No successful campaign or book gets completed without the willing assistance of so many contributors. These contributions come in many forms, shapes, and sizes, including ideas, research, marketing, and sales. Fortunately, my team has been together for many years. They understand me and the way I go about my business. To them, I am most grateful. As for more personalized expressions of thanks, I offer the following:

KENDEL EHRLICH: for your unqualified love and support of all of your husband's projects, I could not do it without you . . .

CHRIS MASSONI: for your devotion, helpfulness, suggestions, patience, and proofreading—you are the best!

GREG MASSONI: for your friendship, loyalty, advice, and steadfast support for all things Ehrlich.

DAVID HAMILTON: for your friendship, support, advice, and willingness to protect my back from detractors of all stripes.

PATRICK MULFORD: for your assistance, suggestions, and research on behalf of this book.

BART MITCHELL: for your friendship, confidence, and support of all things Ehrlich.

ELAINE PEVENSTEIN: for your "Godmother" oversight of all things Ehrlich.

PROFESSOR RICK VATZ: for your steadfast encouragement of this book from Day One.

MAYOR RUDY GIULIANI: for your friendship and support (political and otherwise) over many years and many campaigns.

FRED BARNES: for your encouragement and support of my literary efforts.

JEFF FORMAN: for your thoughts and advice on how to reform and save Social Security.

DENNY MATHER: for your friendship, support, and thoughtful observations about the state of American healthcare.